WRITING
AS
THERAPY

Motivational Activities
for the Developmentally Delayed

THEODORE STAMATELOS
DONALD W. MOTT
Western Carolina Center

 Teachers College, Columbia University
New York and London 1983

Published by Teachers College Press, 1234 Amsterdam Avenue, New York, N.Y. 10027

Library of Congress Cataloging in Publication Data

Stamatelos, Theodore.
  Writing as therapy.

  Bibliography: p.
  Includes index.
  1. Mentally handicapped children—Mental health.
2. Mentally handicapped children—Education—Language
arts.   3. English language—Composition and exercises—
Therapeutic use.   I. Mott, Donald W.   II. Title.
RJ506.My573   1983   618.92′85880651   83-535

ISBN 0-8077-2738-5 (pbk.)

Manufactured in the United States of America

88 87 86 85 84 83   1 2 3 4 5 6

This book is dedicated to all the people with developmental delays whose creative expressions remain locked within them, waiting for the chance to escape and be known.

Contents

Foreword

One of the most difficult tasks special education teachers and clinicians for handicapped persons have in the education and treatment of children and adults is to provide experiences that support their sense of accomplishment and competency. Theodore Stamatelos and his staff in the Fine Arts Department at Western Carolina Center have excelled in their day-to-day work with developmentally delayed people, encouraging their involvement in creative thinking and writing activities. Although this book includes but a portion of their many activities, it succeeds in conveying the essence of their experiences to a reader. Ted Stamatelos and Donald Mott, psychological consultant to the department, suggest that not only is the successful engagement in creative thinking and writing fun for developmentally delayed persons, but it also provides benefits associated with traditional educational and treatment strategies. Behavioral scientists comment that therapy and education have as their goals to change how clients see themselves relative to a personal sense of worth, value, esteem, and a "can-do" approach to life. This book on creative thinking and writing can assist the dedicated professional to look at different and clearly acceptable alternative methods of profitably and positively influencing developmentally delayed individuals' learning and socialization.

Since students themselves do not have to physically write down their words, this book will be especially valuable to teachers of students with a wide range of developmental delays—even those whose students have virtually no "academic skills."

James R. Tompkins, Ph.D.

Acknowledgments

We wish to thank J. Iverson Riddle, M.D., facility director of Western Carolina Center, without whose vision and support of arts for persons with handicaps the work on which this book is based would never have been completed. We also owe a special "thank you" to all the people with developmental delays who have contributed so much to this book and to the excellent staff at Teachers College Press — especially Lois Patton, acquisitions editor, who believed in this book from the beginning. Our thanks also go to David Willenson of Moose Lake State Hospital in Minnesota, for permission to reprint figure 3 in the Appendix.

Additionally, the first author wishes to thank Dr. James R. Tompkins, Dr. Aaron Kramer, Dr. Lucien Buck, Elayne Kardeman, Fran Goldstein, and the Western Carolina Center Fine Arts Department staff for believing in the creative potential of all people; but most of all he thanks Steven and Matthew — who taught him the real meaning of creativity.

Finally, the second author wishes to thank his wife, Kathy, and his two sons, Jonathan and Christopher, for their patience and support; and Elizabeth Miller — whose sense of humor, love of life, and personal dignity have always been an inspiration and a reminder of the humanness of all of us.

WRITING

AS

THERAPY

Motivational Activities
for the Developmentally Delayed

CHAPTER 1

Introduction

Creative art education, or better said, education-through-art, may be especially important not so much for turning out artists or art products, as for turning out better people . . . that they will become full human beings, and that they will move toward actualizing the potentialities that they have. . . . As nearly as I can make out, the only kind of education in existence today that has any faint inkling of such goals is art education . . . it may become the paradigm for all other education.

—A. Maslow (1971)

This book is the product of years of experience, experimentation, and effort in the area of creative writing with a variety of students. The techniques described have been used most often with developmentally delayed youth or emotionally disturbed youth. However, they have also been helpful in work with normal children from three years old and up.

Our creative writing method grew from knowledge of and work in four distinct areas: education, psychology, mental retardation, and the arts. The result is an integrated, transdisciplinary approach that meets a variety of needs. A student not only learns but grows, in a therapeutic sense, as a whole person because of the positive interpersonal nature of the experiences. In addition, the process of the arts ex-

Note: We are aware of the move toward utilizing words like *handicapped* and *developmentally delayed* as adjectives rather than nouns and describing individuals as *persons with developmental delays* or *persons with handicaps* rather than in more dehumanizing terms such as *the handicapped* and *developmentally delayed people*. We have deviated from this policy only when awkward constructions would have resulted.

perience is intrinsically rewarding and enriches the participant by enhancing self-esteem.

It should be emphasized that the primary goal of this creative writing method is not to teach technical writing skills; these are not classes in grammar, spelling, or penmanship. Rather, the goal is to facilitate creative expression. When students express themselves, when they describe feelings, events, or aspects of their lives in their own styles or from their own perspectives, then the goal is met. When a student reads or hears his or her own words, smiles with recognition, and says with delight, "Yes, that's it. That's right! That's exactly what I feel! That's what I want to say!" then the goal is met. It does not matter if the student said "ain't" or "gonna" or "bursted," if the meaning of the writing is clear.

Despite this emphasis on creative or "personal" writing, as opposed to technical writing (Burrows, Ferbie, Jackson, & Sanders, 1952), there is often a serendipitous effect in which the technical skills *do* improve. This improvement usually occurs in a natural manner, as a student enthusiastically tries to find better and better ways to express thoughts and feelings accurately.

Although our creative writing method has been used with a variety of clients of different backgrounds and ages, this book is designed primarily for use by special educators in institutions and public and private schools and by classroom teachers with handicapped students mainstreamed into regular classes. The chapters that follow should enable a teacher to implement creative writing in the classroom. In chapter 2 is a discussion of the philosophical and theoretical foundations on which our creative writing method is based. Chapter 3 then reviews some issues related to evaluating the results of this method. In chapter 4 the specific activities to be used with students are described, with goals, variations, and comments included, so the teacher can tailor them to individual needs. All the activities have been used with mentally retarded persons and have proven to be interesting and effective as educational tasks. They provide a specific, descriptive, step-by-step answer to the oft-heard question regarding arts for handicapped persons, "What arts can we actually *do* with developmentally delayed people, and how?" These activities provide an organized format in which to facilitate communication, establish and nurture positive relationships, and promote a therapeutic milieu. Evidence of the effectiveness of this creative writing method may be seen in chapter 5, which presents a collection of writings by our students. All the writings were generated by developmentally delayed individuals, most of whom reside at Western Carolina Center in Morganton, North Carolina.

For students to benefit most profitably from involvement in creative writing activities, teachers themselves must have a creative attitude. The activities must not be implemented mechanically or inflexibly — as though they are "how to do" recipes. Unfortunately, teaching creatively — with sensitivity and flexibility — is not common practice for many teachers. Torrance (1963) indicates that teachers are not attuned to creativity nor do they see creativity as a goal to be sought. Insinuated within the concepts of special education are many forces that appear to inhibit creativity. Too often, submerged and hidden within the well-meaning efforts of special educators is the pervasive attitude that there is a limit to what handicapped students can learn. The idea of cognitive limitation is not held exclusively by teachers of developmentally disabled people but is shared to a lesser extent by those who teach physically handicapped people. This same attitude is shared in the areas of creativity. Too often, educators reason that creativity is dependent upon cognition: if cognition is limited, therefore creativity is limited.

Handicapped people may well be far more creative than we recognize or understand. To be handicapped often means to adapt in the most creative ways possible for the person. This fact of creative adaptation often goes unnoticed and/or in the case of extreme adaptation is thought of as negative, bizarre, and a deviation from society's concept of "socially acceptable and appropriate." In fact, much concern and attention is given to the retarded person who exhibits *manipulative, noncompliant,* or *inappropriate* behavior. Although many such behaviors (e.g., excessive talking, lying, sexual openness, self-stimulation, feigning illness) are indeed socially deviant and inappropriate according to our values and standards, for the developmentally delayed person they may well be within the realm of normalcy. In addition, they are adaptive and creative from the point of view of meeting a variety of the person's needs. Our concern here is that we try to teach developmentally delayed people more appropriate forms of behaviors to replace the inappropriate ones, but that in the process we do not stifle their natural adaptability, flexibility, creativity, and individualism; nor damage their self-concept through rigid, punitive, excessively demanding, demoralizing, and often futile attempts to remediate the behaviors.

The concept of socially appropriate behavior has led special education down a hopelessly muddy road. Beyond the teaching and valuing of simple social amenities (which the authors advocate) lies the confused state of subjective "appropriateness" that varies from teacher to teacher, school to school, subculture to subculture. We have no desire in this work to get into a discussion of cultural minorities in the schools. Yet it must be understood that handicapped students in the school *are* a minority (and an underprivileged minority) by virtue of their handicapped state. Often the handicapped students appear to be a culturally deprived minority. The imposition of "appropriate sociocultural behavior" often leads to a stifling of expression that in turn too often leads to creative, aesthetic, and cognitive atrophy.

In addition to the issue of social appropriateness, a critical issue in the special education classroom, as in virtually all classrooms, is the degree of control utilized by the teacher. Teachers need control but the structured classroom in which the teacher values control too highly often becomes a rigid, cold classroom where the teacher fears any loss of control and in the process destroys any semblance of creativity. Carl Rogers (1977) has outlined the traditional classroom as follows: authoritarian with a minimum of trust between teacher and student; students controlled in an intermittent state of fear; and the absence of a holistic educational approach that deals with more than the intellect (pp. 69–71). Others such as Farber (1969) see the student as "nigger." In a sense such classrooms are like miniature totalitarian empires where the teacher reigns supreme and the rights and freedoms of the students are few and far between. Of course the justification for this is that the students' best interests are being served, whether they like it or not. To allow greater freedom and control by the students would be too great a risk. We believe the risk is worth taking and that the risks of continuing to *over*-structure and *over*-control and of continuing to fail to facilitate natural expressivity are far greater. If creative writing is to be a meaningful expressive experience, the educator must have the courage to allow handicapped people freedom of expression and to risk inappropriate behavior and a loss of control.

It is obvious from the writings of our students that many of the feelings expressed are deep and frightening. Frightening to the handicapped person, but also to the teacher, parent, psychologist, or other individual to whom they are expressed. There surely is a risk in allowing, even encouraging, the expressions of such deep and troubling feelings, especially in individuals who may not have a great deal of impulse control or ability completely to understand the implications of their own feelings. Certainly though, where such feelings exist in people, whether they are developmentally delayed or not, the feelings *must* ultimately be expressed. We think the risk involved is lessened when such persons are given the opportunity to express themselves in an organized manner in a positive and accepting atmosphere.

Creative writing, like all the arts, is not a passive experience. It is an active experience in that the student brings something of his or her being to the production. Not to accept the spirit of what a student has written is not to accept the student on the most basic human level. In a field that has "regressed" in too many classrooms from an art to a technology, it is no longer merely philosophical to state that creative writing (and all the other art forms) must stand as existential statements. From the Maslowian point of view (refer to chapter 2), such statements are a necessary and integral part of the person's development toward more completeness or self-actualization. Without expressivity and creativity, learning and skill acquisition are without real meaning, simply work for the sake of work, and do not contribute to increased self-esteem or integration of the person. Where expressivity, creativity, and other basic human needs are met, the person is then free to pursue the acquisition of needs higher on the hierarchy, such as learning and skill acquisition.

As is implied so often in this work, education with handicapped people must also be habilitation (as opposed to rehabilitation). *Habilitation* refers to original learning, growth facilitation, the acquisition of new and higher levels of competencies and need satisfaction — in short, the developmental process. Rehabilitation implies that the person once achieved some level, has lost it, and now must regain it. It might be appropriate in some cases to employ rigid, structured techniques in rehabilitation where the skills are known to exist and the problem is primarily one of motivation or commitment. Such techniques are *not* appropriate in a habilitation process, however. Habilitation can *only* occur in a nonthreatening warm environment where the educator accepts the humanness of the students and himself or herself, and recognizes that the primary process is one of *growth* facilitation, not motivation or reinforcement of existing behaviors.

The educator must stimulate and allow the student to "learn to learn."

Unless educators of handicapped people begin enhancing the emotional well-being of their students through acceptance and nurturing relationships that lead to positive self-concepts, they will ultimately fail. Like life, there is more to education than "training" and acquisition of cognitive skills. Too many handicapped students have been turned into "well-behaved" automatons who perform skillfully on demand but who have developed bitterness and hopelessness in what they perceive as a cold and unfair world. One would think from listening and watching many educators that the dispensing of information is the total of education — that education is solely cognitive.

We educators, psychologists, administrators, and the like — in fact, society as a whole — must get away from the notion that art is a luxury. It is well known that music and art are the first school programs to go when budget cuts occur. Creative writing is slightly better received, primarily because it seldom is thought of as an art form. Yet among art educators and artists in general it is becoming clearer and clearer that one of the main values of art is the increase in self-esteem that occurs in the artistic effort. Feelings of self-esteem are critical and fundamental to all people, and art is a facilitator of self-esteem. Maxine Greene, faculty member of the Department of Philosophy and the Social Sciences at Teachers College in New York City, addressed the Arts and the Child Conference in Raleigh, North Carolina, in March 1980. She repeatedly stressed the critical need for art in education and in life. "Without art, we are incomplete," she said, and went on to quote Muriel Rukeyser who wrote: "Fear is not to be feared. Numbness is." Art is not a luxury. It is a necessity.

The educator needs to realize that within the arts process growth and expression of the whole person is facilitated. With this process comes for the teacher the ability to form the genuine relationships that handicapped people so desperately need for self-esteem and, hence, learning. So what is the teacher to do? It is certainly not necessary to throw away all structure or academic goals, but building open, positive relationships and consequently enhancing students' self-esteem must become top priorities in the classroom. Trust students by opening new lines of communication. Accept the statements of handicapped people and in turn be accepted. And where will this lead? It will allow over time handicapped students to experience their own authenticity, their own sense of existence, their uniqueness of being, within the structure of the arts. Let us remember that we are discussing a population singled out because of their disabilities, their non-abilities, their *negative* uniqueness. The person who is handicapped has seldom purposely been singled out for his or her *positive* attributes. Indeed, within the socioeducational structure there is little ability to find positive uniqueness except upon the most superficial level: receiving an "A" on an examination may indicate achievement but hardly uniqueness. The arts, however, enhance both uniqueness and achievement, enabling all people—including those with handicaps—to experience a sense of being alive and to express this in their acts. What more fitting way can there be to begin habilitation than to exclaim you are alive?

CHAPTER 2

Philosophical and Theoretical Foundations

This chapter presents the important philosophical and theoretical bases of our creative writing method. After defining the term humanism, we point out some of the benefits that occur in the classroom when using a humanistic approach such as our creative writing method. Then we summarize the theoretical aspects of personality development of developmentally delayed people. Next, we discuss the importance of the creative process in education for all people and describe what actually occurs in that process. This is followed by a discussion of the importance of creativity specifically for handicapped people. Finally, the ingredients necessary for a creative approach to teaching in general are described with an emphasis on the specific ramifications of utilizing such an approach when creative writing is implemented.

OVERVIEW OF HUMANISM

The teacher who implements the creative writing method outlined in this book will undoubtedly recognize the therapeutic and habilitative benefits that occur, as reflected in many of the poignant and powerful writings by students in chapter 5. Those writings reflect the human qualities of the students and the degree to which their expressions were valued within the creative writing process. Both the recognition of "human" qualities and the valuing of those qualities are intrinsic to the humanistic philosophy on which the creative writing method is based.

We define *humanism* as follows: humanism is a philosophical orientation and theoretical approach to the understanding of man that stresses the inner potential of human beings to grow in all spheres of development (e.g., emotional, behavioral, physiological, spiritual, and social); the reality of the phenomenal world in which man lives; and the importance of consciousness in enabling each human being to share in the shaping of his or her own destiny (Stamatelos & Mott, 1982b). For the purposes of this work, *humanism* refers to the humanistic school of psychology, as represented by the writings of Rogers (1951, 1961), Maslow (1971), and Jourard (1974), among many others. Humanistic psychology is often described as the "third force" in psychology, a descriptive term indicating humanistic psychology's history of being a reaction to the psychoanalytic and behavioristic schools of psychology. The word *humanism* also is connected with theological humanism. While a recognition of the philosophic roots of humanistic psychology in theological humanism is accurate, it is important to distinguish between the two. Humanistic psychology does not imply an antitheistic or aspiritual position; in fact, the importance of the spiritual aspects of humanity have been incorporated into humanistic psychology. Humanism also must be distinguished from *humanitarianism*. Humanitarianism involves anything that benefits people. Humanism may be humanitarian when it improves the lives of people, but many other philosophies may also be humanitarian in their implementation. Simply stated, humanism must be distinguished from humanitarianism in that humanism is a philosophy about people, that is concerned with the nature and potential of people; while humanitarianism is a concern with deeds that are done *for* people, regardless of philosophical orientation.

A critical aspect of humanism is the utilization of *phenomenological* material expressed by people. Humanism asserts that human issues can only be fully dealt with when a human perspective is taken, specifically when an effort is made to understand reality as it is perceived by man. Attitudes, values, emotions, and beliefs, as well as physiological perceptions, as they are expressed verbally or nonverbally by the individual, are considered both significant and necessary "data" from a humanistic perspective. The Human beings are thought of as *conscious* beings, whose consciousness of themselves as well as the world around them, makes them unique among living creatures. The idea of *self* is an important aspect of consciousness and issues such as self-concept and self-esteem are critical to humanism. (See Rychlak, 1976, for a discussion of the self in humanistic theory.)

Expressions of the phenomenological field by the individual are accepted as *authentic* for that person at that point in time. Simply stated, the phenomenological field can be defined as the interpretation by an individual of the experiences he or she perceives. The notion of authenticity implies a recognition that the individual's viewpoints, values, and so forth must be *accepted* as part of that individual and no one has the right or ability to dispute them. Ideally, relationships between people are built through a process of sharing perceptions, during which each person strives to know and understand one's self and the other person in a manner as close to "reality" as possible. Total objectivity, however, is not sought, because it is not considered theoretically possible. What is sought are *peak experiences* in which the individual becomes fully involved in creative and transcendent "here-now" processes. *Existential statements* of the individual's perception of his or her own existence as a unique, valuable human being reflect the importance of being alive. The ability to make such statements, to be alive and aware of one's self as a unique, functioning, and valuable individual contribute to *self-actualization:* becoming all that one is able to become. Self-actualization involves a recognition that human beings can exert control over their own lives; that they are more than machines or animals lacking in consciousness; that they are capable of ongoing growth and development in all aspects of their being; that they are able to transcend the limits imposed upon them by "external reality" to become more than the sum of their physiology and environmental history would predict. Humanism recognizes the causal effects of day-to-day experiences, but emphasizes the ability of human beings to interpret, conceptualize and, organize those experiences in light of their own values and aspirations and then to act in manners consistent with their inner selves.

HABILITATIVE ARTS THERAPY

This creative writing method is one of several aspects of treatment that involve handicapped people with the arts. We have coined the term *habilitative arts therapy* to describe these treatments, all of which are grounded in humanism. It is essential that the fundamentals of habilitative arts therapy be understood, so that this creative writing method will be utilized within the proper frame of reference.

Habilitative arts therapy (HAT) is a client-centered approach that utilizes various art modalities to facilitate growth and development among participants. An important distinction is made between HAT and the use of the arts for other purposes such as recreation (e.g., arts and crafts) or art therapy. Although it is recognized that HAT stimulates much emotional material, as well as projection, it is *not* psychoanalytically oriented and hence differs significantly from traditional art therapy.

A most important element of HAT is the emphasis on the whole person. A holistic approach is taken, in which attention is paid to social, emotional, cognitive, physiological, behavioral, and environmental factors. A range of experiences are provided in an effort to involve the total being of each person. Stress is made on such fundamentals as body rhythms, breathing, body concept, and overall self-image and self-esteem. An overt effort is made to facilitate peak experience in the lives of clients.

Also of great importance is the emphasis in HAT on the establishment of positive nurturing relationships between the habilitative art therapist and the client as well as between and among the clients. Rogers' writings on client-centered therapy in general (1951, 1954a) and on education (1969) have been particularly important in the development of HAT.

Another critical area is the emphasis on decision making and control by the clients. To the greatest extent possible each client is allowed to exert influence on the activities that take place. Although basic ground rules are set (e.g., property damage or aggression are not allowed) and the therapist may exert some control on the overall activity (e.g., painting vs. music vs. creative writing, and so forth), the client is encouraged and expected to make many choices within these parameters. The need to make choices is a basic psychological need as well as a human right that we believe has been neglected within the field of mental retardation. Further discussion of this point can be found in Mott, Rosenkoetter, and Stamatelos (1981).

Finally, a fundamental of HAT is its stress on the *process* that occurs rather than the product that results. *HAT is not concerned directly with teaching skills or with the creation of products.* Instead the primary concern is the establishment of a positive and trusting atmosphere in which active engagement of the individual in the expression of his or her phenomenological field is facilitated. Empathetic reflections of the expressions of each individual are made, assuring each person that his or her views are accepted as *authentic*. The notion of authenticity of the phenomenological field is critical. It assumes positive regard for the student by the therapist and facilitates positive self-regard within each student. The *authenticity* of each student's expressions *cannot* and *should not* be questioned in a humanistic milieu. Hence, "failure" within the HAT milieu does not occur. Despite this effort to make HAT a positive experience that emphasizes the *process* of expression, products of increasing quality do emerge as students become more aware of their own expressivity and more motivated to clarify their communication. Serendipitous gains in many other areas also occur, including gains in such diverse areas as socialization, perceptual-motor coordination, verbal skills, impulse control, cognitive abilities, art-specific abilities, and so on. It is critical, however, that these gains are recognized as serendipitous by-products of the *process,* which always stresses authentic expressions of a person's inner perceptions of self and the world around.

The five primary art modalities utilized within HAT include visual arts (painting, sculpting, and so forth), music, drama, creative writing, and movement and dance. All these modalities are utilized at the appropriate level of complexity and involvement for each individual. Most frequently an *integrated* approach is taken, in which a combination of two or more art modalities is utilized to stimulate expression by students. The integrated approach serves to facilitate more complete involvement of the whole person and increases the likelihood of engaging the individual in some activity at which he or she will find some success.

To summarize, the basic goals of HAT may be outlined as follows:

Increasing Self-Concept
Sense of self as an entity separate from the environment

Sense of the location of the body in space
Sense of self as a specific conscious ideation
Physical image of one's self
One's name
One's body parts
Gender concepts
Growth experiences
Feelings of warmth or positive regard from others
Feelings of noncontingent positive regard from others
Sense of self-esteem
Sense of personal values
    One's immediate preferences
    One's day-to-day preferences
    One's long-range preferences
    One's individual vs. group preferences
    One's own mutually exclusive preferences
    One's willingness to take personal risks
Facilitating Exploration
    Of one's self
    Of one's physical environment
    Imaginative problem-solving
    Actual problem-solving
    Fantasizing and imagining
Facilitating Expression
    Rhythmic patterns
    Language skills
        Vocabulary
        Spatial concepts (big/little; in/out/under)
        Others' names
        Colors
        Shapes
    Musical expression
    Graphic arts, photography, and so forth
    Creative writing
    Affective expression (verbal or nonverbal)
    Affective vocabulary
Facilitating Appropriate Socialization
    Parallel play
    Mutual play
    Group activity (play or problem-solving)

Role identification (self-roles)
Role identification (others' roles)
Ability to identify one's own affects
Ability to identify others' affects
Expression of sexuality
Sense of social expectations
Sense of social responsibility
Sense of social styles, mores, values, customs, and so forth
Developing Autonomy
Ability to engage in individual problem-solving
Perception of ability to control self
Perception of ability to control others and environment
Ability to make decisions affecting one's self
Ability to accept responsibility for the outcomes of one's actions
Improving Motor Control
General body control
Fine motor control
Gross motor control
Proper breathing
Physical balance
Movement in performing arts (e.g., dance, drama)
Mutual movement and/or group movement
Increasing Academic/Cognitive Skills
Number concepts
Knowledge of art concepts
Language skills

THERAPEUTIC ASPECTS OF CREATIVE WRITING

The reader has probably noticed the similarity between the essential principles of humanism and habilitative arts therapy. The similarity is natural because we stress the therapeutic benefits of HAT. However, we believe that any good classroom environment organized according to humanistic principles should be therapeutic. Consequently, the terms *education* and *therapy* are used interchangeably throughout this book, as are the words *client* and *student*, as well as *teacher* and *therapist*.

The emphasis on learning specific information, gaining new skills, or progressing from one developmental level to the next is valid *only* when the ultimate goal of these endeavors is kept uppermost in the minds of those involved. That goal being the enrichment, or self-actualization, of the life of the learner in all its aspects — social and emotional, as well as cognitive. Though one can learn in an environment that is *not* generally enriching and conducive to growth in all areas of personality, the process of teaching is much more enjoyable and efficient in the long run when the classroom is fun, motivating, and marked by mutual respect and acceptance between students and teacher. To the extent that the techniques described in this book help to produce a generally motivating, enjoyable, respectful environment, they are of value. Their value increases many times over, however, because of several specific therapeutic effects facilitated by the exercises.

The creative writing program we describe in this book has multiple therapeutic functions. First, communication between the teacher and student is enhanced through the utilization of "reflective" techniques. This builds rapport and establishes a firm foundation of trust upon which to base both further creative writing experiences and other classroom activities. Second, the student's self-image is improved and becomes more positive with each successful activity. Self-acceptance is learned as he is accepted by teachers and peers. Third, because of feelings of security based on trust in the relationships of acceptance, the general skill level of the student in other areas is improved. Academic as well as social skills are likely to blossom. Finally, the writing helps the student to reveal aspects of self in increasing depths of significance. As sublimated drives and needs are expressed symbolically through the writing, the student is better able to understand feelings and exert self-control. This internal growth and motivation is reflected symbolically, and facilitated, in the creative process. The writing tends to increase in both affective and cognitive maturity and profundity, often taking on great meaning to all involved.

In a therapeutic situation, the first step is establishment of an empathic relationship, but, again according to Rogers, a person can only become *self-actualized*, or fulfilled to greatest capacity, when noncontingent acceptance of self, as a good, valuable, and worthwhile human being, is learned. This self-acceptance can only develop when one is accepted noncontingently by a significant other. The creative writing exercises promote this since the student and his or her work are valued noncontingently by the teacher (a significant other). Although growth and improvement are desired and actively sought, they are the *mutual* and natural goals met through the process that is always positive. Hence students learn to accept and like themselves as well as gradually to produce better and better work. They increase their self-knowledge, self-acceptance, knowledge of writing techniques, and creativity all at the same time.

In the typical classroom—whether designed for handicapped or nonhandicapped students or heterogeneous groupings—many activities, if not most, place contingencies on the student. Grades are contingent on performance. Privileges are contingent on completion of tasks. Acceptance (or the freedom from expulsion) is contingent on acceptable behavior, especially in special education classrooms. (How many children have been accepted into public school special education classrooms or mainstreamed into regular classrooms *contingent* on "appropriate" behavior?) Each rejection, each failure, is a blow to the individual's emotional need for self-acceptance and security.

It is not the intent of this book to do away with all contingencies in classrooms. But it is necessary, purposefully and specifically, to seek out ways to balance the often-overwhelming effects of frequent sterilization and mechanization of the interactions between teacher and student that often thwart the student's sense of individuality, self-worth, and belonging; and in our opinion, his or her ability to achieve desired goals in general. The creative writing techniques described in this book give the teacher specific, constructive, organized, relevant, and enjoyable ways in which to offer his or her students at least one classroom activity that promotes overall mental health as well as cognitive development. The more secure students feel in their relationships and their general environments, the more interested will they become in pursuing activities higher on the hierarchical ladder. This is true for all students, whether handicapped or not.

There is a critical aspect of creative writing that separates it from other activities such as recreational and freetime activities, which are typically more fun and less mechanized than usual classroom academic training. Although creative writing meets security needs, is noncontingent, and deals with affective components, it also teaches skills, since it fosters creativity, flexibility, and freedom of mind. Each exercise is specifically designed to enhance and stimulate learning in the student. Even as we believe that education should not take place in the absence of a nurturant, healthy environment, we also hold that education should and *can* take place in an emotionally healthy environment. Lucien A. Buck and Aaron Kramer (1976) state in an article entitled "Poetic Creativity in Deaf Children":

> Implicit here is a balance between the free play of thought (openness to the world and one's own imagination) and technical skill. An incessant dialectic between these two polarities has . . . been proposed by some investigators as a foundation for creative productions. Justifications of creative potential in the deaf, therefore, requires the demonstration of technical skills as well as an open imagination. (p. 32)

Just as "incessant dialectic" is necessary in work with deaf children, it is necessary in our view in work with anyone.

The creative writing setting, as well as being conducive to learning writing skills, is conducive to acquisition and enhancement of social skills. The class group is encouraged to share and interact in the process of self-exploration, self-expression, and learning. Even as each student feels accepted by the teacher and learns self-acceptance, he or she also learns to accept the others in the class and feels accepted by them. Marvin Blumberg (1976) has found that group work with mentally retarded individuals in the area of "creative dramatics" enhances social skills: "These individuals need help to develop broader vistas; they need an opening of the imagination and courage for new dreams to strengthen their egos and to transform them into social beings" (p. 17). Fashioned to some extent after Moreno's psychodrama, Blumberg's technique fostered writing skills as well as performance and role playing. Creative writing can be particularly beneficial as a catalyst for socialization between handicapped students and other students in regular classrooms. Because all students participate as equals, whose products are valued nonjudgmentally, there is a sense of egalitarianism that often results. Our experiences in heterogeneous groupings have been extremely positive, and we have observed communication and developing of friendships between individuals who otherwise had little opportunity for true mutuality.

As students learn more and more skills, and as they trust themselves, their peers, and their teacher at increasing levels, the significance of their work increases. It has been said that all art forms must have an affective component — they must express feelings. As students engage

in the processes described in this book, they learn to express and record feelings about themselves and their environments. Feelings they
may have never understood before or have acknowledged before are
expressed. As their fulfillment and gratification at expressing themselves and at creating a product increases, their desires increase to
both express themselves and accurately record their feelings. This
motivates them to succeed in both technical and affective realms. Several other writers have reported this phenomenon in work with various populations, including schizophrenic persons (Buck & Kramer,
1977), deaf children (Buck & Kramer, 1977), elderly persons (Koch,
1978), and persons with mental retardation (Blumberg, 1976).

PERSONALITY ISSUES

Recognizing the role of motivation and the importance of expression, self-esteem, and other emotional needs in working with developmentally delayed people implies that they are essentially similar to
normal persons in their emotional development. For a review of literature pertaining to this area, see Mott, Rosenkoetter, and Stamatelos
(1981). In particular, the empirical research of Ed Zigler, of Yale University, provides a solid foundation for viewing the retarded individual
as a whole person, with emotional development essentially like nonretarded persons. Zigler (1973) says: "It would be more parsimonious to
view the development of the personality of the retarded as no different
in nature than the development of personality in individuals of normal intellect" (p. 240). However, as described in Mott et al. (1981, p.
6), Zigler (1966) does point out that his work has suggested

> several tendencies which frequently occur in individuals with men-
> tal retardation who undergo institutionalization or other social de-
> priving experiences: increased desire for attention and approval
> by adults; higher positive reaction tendencies, as well as higher
> negative reaction tendency; increased wariness of adults; lower ex-
> pectation of success; greater outer directedness.

Consequently, it is imperative that treatment approaches be based on
an awareness of the individual students' personalities, as well as their
academic and social histories. Such a holistic approach will yield ben-

efits not only in cognitive areas but in affective areas as well. Though Zigler's work relates specifically to mentally retarded individuals, our experience strongly indicates that his points are valid for all developmentally delayed persons.

One of the major benefits of our creative writing method is that it facilitates expression. This is critical because *all* persons have the need to express themselves and to be understood. In serving individuals with developmental delays, we believe it is necessary to learn to perceive the world as they perceive it — as much as that is possible. To accomplish this, we must enable such persons to learn to express themselves. As described in Mott et al. (1981),

> a fruitful method of approach may well be one which incorporates a phenomenological perspective. In fact, science as a whole, and quantum physics specifically (which is the vanguard of science) no longer rely totally on a traditionally "objective" analysis of data-based research (e.g., Zukav, 1979). Rather, in the phenomenological position, the observer is a participant in the phenomenological field of action (see Goldman, 1978 for a discussion of "participant observation" in human services research). Phenomenological investigation within the field of mental retardation is almost nonexistent. However, although not explicitly stated, some researchers' recent work reflects this view (e.g., Zigler, 1973; DeVillis, 1977). A phenomenological approach would reveal and/or elicit existential acts by persons who have mental retardation, which would help us create a conceptual framework through which we may better understand their development. We would then be in a better position to facilitate improvements in self concept, as well as other significant personality variables. (p. 10)

One of the obstacles to implementing a phenomenological approach with mentally retarded or other developmentally delayed people is the fact that they often are inhibited in their expressions. As we stressed in chapter 1, this inhibition occurs not primarily because of cognitive difficulties but because many developmentally delayed people have learned that it is not always safe or productive to express themselves. Recent evidence suggests that many handicapped people may exhibit "learned helplessness," which is actually a form of depression. In essence, because of repeated failure and repeated experiences in relatively unresponsive environments, many handicapped people learn to rely on others to meet their needs. Additionally, they learn to suppress many of their expressions, desires, fantasies, wishes, and hopes. They learn, in essence, to minimize interactions with the world in which they initiate the process. These issues and their relationship to habilitative arts therapy are described at length in Stamatelos and Mott (1982c). One of the major points made in that paper is that handicapped people often virtually stop exploring their environment. In essence, their creativity, their exploration, their ability to play, may be damaged or destroyed. This does not have to be the case.

PLAY AND CREATIVITY

Many have identified the free play of children as the impetus for both creative and cognitive growth. There is even evidence to assume that creative activity begins in infancy, that "manipulatory and exploratory" behavior in infants is creative thinking (Schachtel, 1971; Torrance, 1963).

It is believed that free play of the very young is the way in which children explore their universe, imitating the actions and character traits of those around them (Schachtel, 1971). McCaslin (1974) concludes that free play of the very young is the earliest expression in dramatic form but must not be confused with drama (p. 5). It should be added that dramatic expression is also the earliest expression of creativity in the area of the arts. The educator may capitalize from such naturally occurring free play and dramatic expression to provide experiences for the student that are both creative and educational. Play in young children may well be the incubator that nurtures schemes that could become goals for children in both the special and normal classroom. "We want them [children] to become involved in experience that will lead to imaginating, exploring, reasoning, inventing, experimenting, and selecting so that these experiences will not only be rich in themselves but lead to personal creative growth" (Linderman & Herberholtz, 1964, p. x).

For the educator of the developmentally delayed child, the observation of creativity may not be as clear as the literature may suggest, for with the severely retarded and seriously disturbed child, creativity may take a form of behavior that the educator finds inappropriate or objectionable. "The playroom behavior of immature and neurotic children is characterized by excess of inhibition or aggression" (Ginott, 1961, p. 40).

The concepts of play and creativity do not mean a structureless situation in the classroom. The educator can structure the play situation and guide it to achieve both a fun situation and a learning experience without the loss of spontaneity so essential for play and creative responses.

With children who are physically handicapped the limitations to play are usually obvious. The creative instructor normally has little difficulty in circumnavigating these limitations. It is with retarded children and emotionally disturbed children that administering techniques for creative responses often meet with difficulty.

Persons with mental retardation are frequently characterized as concrete learners, and in cognitive areas this appears to us to be accurate. However, as has been indicated earlier, retarded people may be quite creative in play or in other affective areas. Though creativity and cognitive skills often overlap, they are not one and the same operation. It is not as difficult as is widely believed to engage retarded children in creative games, although patience and sensitivity are necessary since the process may take longer to initiate. The importance of play, creativity, and exploration in a client-centered approach to education has been described thoroughly in *Freedom to Learn* by Carl Rogers (1969).

Children with severe emotional problems may not have the internal control to fantasize appropriately without the involvement of their own severe disorders. A firmer structure should be initiated with this population of students, one in which the boundaries of content are defined clearly. With emotionally disturbed children, fantasy play should be firmly structured around reality situations that are important in the students' lives. When a teacher feels certain a child knows the behavioral parameters, less-structured fantasy play can be encouraged.

THE BASICS OF CREATIVITY

At this point, a clear understanding of the basic factors leading to creativity is needed. Research studies into the origins of creativity have indicated specific stages that occur during the process of the creative act (Parnes, 1972). Though various models of the creative process exist (Arieti, 1976), the following multistage development of creative responses embodies tested techniques that must be incorporated into special education for handicapped people to ensure their productivity.

SENSITIVITY.   Experiences in touch, smell, sound, and so forth contribute to the person's understanding of self and environment. Such awareness is essential in the creative process as well as in education in general. Sensitivity and incubation work hand in hand to allow synergistic experiences to occur.

INCUBATION.   Creativity cannot be forced. It must be allowed. Everyone has experienced frustration trying to remember or accomplish something to no avail. Only when they gave up and stopped consciously thinking about it, did their subconscious processing allow the answer to occur.

SYNERGY.   Synergy is the unique combination of two or more parts that together create a new product that is more than the sum of the parts. For example, for a young child, a synergistic experience can be the creation of a collage from a collection of sticks, leaves, and paper. The parts lose their identity in the creation of the whole. Words are used synergistically when they are formulated to create a new conception. For example, Sandburg's famous line, "The fog comes on little cat feet."

SERENDIPITY.   Similar to synergy, serendipity is the phenomenon that occurs when a new or additional product emerges unintentionally from some process. It is different from synergy in that the new product has its own identity and meaning separate from the intended goal or product. A person may learn a dance intentionally and serendipitously develop greater fine and gross motor control in general.

To sum up, sensitivity and incubation combine to allow synergistic experiences that yield serendipitous products. Thus, the fourfold process of creativity occurs.

CREATIVITY IN HANDICAPPED CHILDREN

Unfortunately, the area of creative growth has often been neglected in special classrooms. With the often-overwhelming problems that handicapped students may display, creativity often takes a second place to academic or self-help skills. Many teachers and administrators feel that creative growth is a secondary phenomenon that is acquired at a higher level of cognition and therefore has little place within the curriculum of the cognitively delayed child.

Creativity is closely linked to the ability to symbolize, which is an abstract process. Based on our experiences not only are developmentally delayed persons able to be creative, they are also able to express abstract concepts, especially on the subconscious level. However, as we have discussed in a separate paper (Stamatelos & Mott, 1982a), the opposite view has traditionally been accepted:

> There has been an assumption that the retarded person cannot deal with abstract concepts. In fact, in our experience, that has been one description that has sometimes been used to explain or operationally define mental retardation. Consequently, a great deal of attention has been placed on concrete or overt behavior . . . the retarded person has been viewed and analyzed mechanistically and over-simplistically in terms of her overt behavior. While it is probably true that retarded individuals (especially severely or profoundly retarded) do not cognitively understand their own internal processes, the processes still occur. . . . The concept of abstraction is critical here because the retarded individuals' behaviors, whether verbal or non-verbal, are . . . the symbolic representation of inner processing. (pp. 24–25)

The myth that only intelligent people can be creative must be dispelled. Recent studies of intelligence and creativity report the correlation between the two to be low (Lowenfeld & Brittain, 1964). In fact, there is evidence to suppose that retarded people paint in a *more* "abstract, unique and imaginative style" than people of average intelligence (Stabler, Stabler, & Karger, 1977). Despite this, it is a mistake to assume that creativity will emerge on its own without the guidance of a sensitive educator and a carefully structured environment. Gaitskell and Hurwitz (1975) say: "We still have the laissez-faire teachers with us and, paradoxically, there are none more dictatorial than they.

Even if the children require instruction, they insist on withholding it from them and maintain that they will learn without urging or guidance" (p. 39).

Most special educators have developed their expertise in the areas of cognitive development. It is therefore not surprising that most and, in some cases, all goals set for individual students are addressed to the cognitive realm of development. Burkhart and McNeil (1968) have pointed out that teachers are often resistive to the creative process in their students and see it as opposed to the process necessary for the acquisition of cognitive skills.

> Creativity is often associated with rebellion, delinquency and social disruption. Studies of creative people tend to support this notion by showing that creativity is associated with preference for change rather than stability; tendency to delay closure rather than to structure ideas; tendency to challenge old structure; tendency to let incoming perceptions dictate their own patterns, rather than to force preconceived patterns on them and so on. Opposed to these tendencies are the overwhelmingly dominant tendencies of most people to maintain structure and to find security in maintenance of an unchanging environment. This tendency is deep-seated in the facts of human adjustment. It is perfectly natural, then, for most people to resent those who are unstructured and who are responsive to freshness and differences because they are threats to security. (p. xviii)

Burkhart and McNeil view most teachers as highly structured individuals whose main concern has been with subject rather than "process," which the creative act would imply.

For the handicapped child (as for average children) creative pursuits as part of the classroom milieu can bring to view environmental awareness in personally expressive terms. It involves the investment on the part of the student in affective behavior, which is often inhibited or displayed confusedly by a handicapped student.

A primary ingredient in any program that professes to embrace creative acts must be an expectation that ingredients of an affective nature will be present in the process. All arts to one degree or another have an affective component. It is the unfolding and use of affect in the process of creative writing that demarks it from simple language arts exercises.

Burrows et al. (1952) have defined two styles of writing of which the educator should become aware. They make a distinction between *practical* and *personal* writing. Practical writing meets practical communication needs; it requires adherence to grammar, spelling, syntax, and handwriting. Correctness of practical written material is held in high value. In personal writing, affective responses and personal ideas about the world have free reign. Within this mode of writing, the teacher must allow for the spontaneity of ideas and true expression. Personal writing is the basis of creative writing as an artform as opposed to writing as a pedantic exercise. It is within the mode of *personal writing* that the educator must unconditionally accept the production of the child. Grammar, spelling, handwriting, and syntax should not be of concern during *personal writing assignments*.

Among expert opinion, it is suggested that young children go through a developmental stage where they enjoy what Pease (1964) calls "scribble writing": random, nonorganized lines in artistic production. It is also suggested that children engage in scribbling and the beginning of writing just for self-expression (Pilulski, 1975). Lowenfeld and Brittain (1964) place the emphasis on motoric pleasure at the earliest stage of creative development. It would appear that at early stages of development motoric and self-expressive schemes are inexplicably connected.

In handicapped children with disabilities of a developmental nature, the relationship between self-expression and motoric pleasure must be kept in the forefront of considerations for the teacher who will succeed in establishing a creative environment for the student and ultimately in facilitating the production of creative writing in the classroom. For low-functioning handicapped children, motoric stimulation on various levels will be a key factor for involving them in creative behavior.

Many of the activities to stimulate creative responses suggested later in this book are motoric in nature — involving integration of artistic modalities designed to create a pleasurable experience as well as to stimulate expression. Though the ultimate concern of this work is to deal with creating writing tasks in the classroom ("personal writing"), it would be ludicrous to separate this creative behavior from other art modalities and to assume that creative writing is inherently of a different nature from other art forms. Creative writing is not and should not be considered exclusively exercises in language arts usage since it is not purely an expository mode but rather reaches beyond subject limitation to new areas of inventiveness. No mode of writing is pure (Kantor & Perron, 1977), and personal writing is no exception. It should ultimately incorporate the rules of language but be recognized as an art form in the same way that calligraphy is an art form but dependent on the structure of letters and words.

Literature is an art form because it deals with the human condition. It is not simply ideas and language usage that places literature among the arts but that it is insinuated with feelings and emotions: particular and personal views of the life condition. The greatest of authors have imbued their work with a depth of emotion to which we may all respond in a like manner. Furthermore, the artists of literature are not imprisoned within the confines of linguistic rules; Joyce, Stein, and Cummings, most notable among a host of others, have manipulated language for their own use. The rules of language are important for communication, but they are not sacred.

For handicapped children who more often than not have had their perceptions locked within them, creative writing may be the only opportunity they have to appropriately expose their feelings.

> As a means for self-expression, writing helps children to deal with fantasy and emotion. Through this medium, they can also learn to sort out and order their experiences, and to discover and share universal feelings . . . our states of tension — especially unhappy tensions — become tolerable as we manage to state what is wrong — to get it said — whether to a sympathetic friend, or on paper to a hypothetical sympathetic reader, or even to one's self. (Hayakawa, 1964, pp. 145–146)

The ability of developmentally delayed persons to express abstract concepts is evident in many of the samples of creative writing contained in chapter 5.

THE CREATIVE TEACHER

The teacher who embraces the concepts of creativity in the classroom establishes a creative relationship with his or her students. E. Paul Torrance (1963) states: "The term creative relationship seems appropriate because the desired kind of relationship takes place in much the same way as does creative thinking. The creative relationship between the teacher and pupil requires a willingness on the part of the teacher to permit one thing to lead to another, to embark with the child on an unknown adventure" (p. 17).

Torrance (1963) continues to state various ways in which we may reward and reinforce creative behavior in the classroom:

1. Be respectful of the unusual questions children ask
2. Be respectful of the unusual ideas and solutions displayed by children
3. Show children that their ideas have value and are valued by us
4. Provide opportunities and give credit for self-initiated learning by children
5. Provide chances for children to learn, think, and discover without immediate evaluation
6. Evoke originality in thinking by making it clear that such thinking is expected

It is also important for the teacher to understand that in the creative process there is *not just one answer* involved. The educator must be aware of the multiplicity of possible responses. Too often we discuss the "stimulating environment" without discussing the "responsive environment." It is as if we stimulate the environment to manipulate only one response that we have decided (ahead of time) is the correct response. In a truly stimulating situation the educator must expect and respect a multiplicity of divergent responses from the student.

Table 2.1 contrasts student-centered and teacher-centered approches to creative writing. It should be kept in mind that this illustration applies equally to many other creative classroom experiences as well.

Carl Rogers (1954b) has written that there are two conditions that are necessary to nurture creativity: *psychological safety* and *psychological freedom*. An educator who allows a class freedom of expression within the confines of a safe stable environment has taken a large step toward nurturing creativity within the classroom.

TABLE 2.1   CONTRASTING APPROACHES TO CREATIVE WRITING

Student-Centered	Teacher-Centered
1. Most students are fearful of new experiences. They are eased into creative writing by the teacher's making it seem fun and providing a secure situation.	The teacher gives assignment and insists that creative writing task follows. It is sink or swim.
2. Teacher displays enjoyment of the creative writing activity. Creative writing is presented as a positive value.	Creative writing is considered just one more area the teacher is forced to teach.
3. A nonjudgmental environment is established in which creative responses are encouraged.	The teacher looks for and insists on a specific point of view in the student's work. The class is given formulas that must be followed.
4. The psychological environment allows for freedom of expression. The physical environment in which creative writing occurs is one that is structured yet stimulating.	The environment is over stimulating or barren. Other activities are occurring which are distracting to the student.
5. The teacher views creative writing not as the teaching of handwriting or spelling but as a mode in which to elicit creative thinking. (Many teachers find it preferable to make creative writing a verbal activity in which they take down the creative piece by dictation or with a tape recorder. Obviously, verbal activities provide those students with no academic skills with a way to be creative.)	Creative writing tasks can "kill many birds with one stone." Spelling, handwriting, and sentence structure is stressed during creative writing time.
6. By searching with a student for the precise meaning of a creative work, the teacher elicits self-criticism of the work. The teacher then guides the student until he or she sees how it can be improved.	All creative writing is graded.

Student-Centered	*Teacher-Centered*
7. The teacher realizes that each student has something valuable and creative to share no matter how limited it may appear and relates this to the student.	The teacher ignores or criticizes individuality or creative expressions of many students.
8. Each student possesses his or her own collection of work in a book.	After a product is finished, it is filed away.
9. To the teacher each piece of creative writing stands on its own as an individual and valuable work of the student.	The teacher gives higher marks to or praises work he or she likes best.
10. The teacher reads to the class the work of all students, unless the student for reasons of privacy, should object.	The teacher reads to class only the "best" work created.
11. The teacher sees value in writing as a way to integrate other disciplines and modalities of learning with the total educational experience.	The teacher sees creative writing as not related to other activities of learning.
12. The teacher uses creative writing as a means to better understand the student.	The teacher does not see creative writing as a way of establishing a meaningful relationship with the student.
13. The teacher reinforces the beauty and creativity intrinsic to language.	The teacher does not view language as creative but as set formulas for communication.

CHAPTER 3

Methods of Evaluation

This chapter deals with various issues related to evaluating or measuring the results of implementing our creative writing method. Although the essence of creative writing is the *process*, much growth and serendipitous learning occur, as described earlier. We feel the writings speak for themselves as the major "data" resulting from this creative writing method. We recognize, however, the need of many teachers to provide other forms of data to account for their time spent in activities such as creative writing. This chapter is intended to provide the necessary guidelines to enable teachers to document the growth that occurs in their students.

First, some philosophical questions regarding evaluation in general are discussed. Of particular concern are the questions of "authenticity" and "objectivity." Next we present various dimensions of measurement that we have found to be relevant in working with clients in general. Then examples of specific types of evaluation methods are given, followed by a discussion of the importance of carefully choosing the specific goals to be evaluated in individual situations. Finally the issues of evaluation are put into perspective, given the philosophical position taken in this book and the value system implied in that philosophical position.

PHILOSOPHICAL ISSUES

As stated previously in this book, we believe a major value of our creative writing method is its ability to deal with the whole person, using a broad-based, humanistic approach. Individual skills such as language concepts or overt social behaviors do emerge through creative writing, and these can be evaluated through a variety of traditional educational approaches with which teachers are generally familiar. Some techniques we feel are appropriate are described later in this chapter. In implementing this creative writing method it is critical, however, to emphasize the broader, more abstract personality variables such as self-esteem, self-control, belongingness, values clarification, and so on. Whenever one tries to measure such broad issues, serious questions regarding "objectivity" are raised. Specifically, the concepts of *validity* (i.e., does the data measure what it was designed to measure?) and *reliability* (i.e., how consistently does the data measure what it was designed to measure?) are crucial.

As an example of the difficulties of obtaining objective data in evaluating the more abstract constructs, let us consider the critical area of self-concept. In her book, *The Self Concept,* Ruth C. Wylie (1961) discusses the difficulties in measuring variables related to self-concept. In reviewing the literature in that area, she presents a table of the instruments that had been used to measure self-concept. She comments that "for two thirds of all instruments in the table no reliability information is available in published sources. For 80% of all instruments refered to in the table, no information on construct validity for inferring the phenomenal self is available in published sources" (p. 88). Though Wylie's book is over twenty years old, it illustrates the dilemma of obtaining accurate measurements of abstract though critical constructs such as self-concept—a dilemma that still exists today, especially among developmentally delayed populations. There still are few objective instruments or procedures available to measure self-concept in developmentally delayed persons, especially persons who are severely or profoundly retarded. This situation was summed up by Rosenkoetter (1980):

> The literature relating self-concept to the mentally retarded is characterized by disparity, contradictions, tenuous results, and invalid conclusions. A preoccupation with substantive issues before more basic methodological considerations have been adequately considered lies at the core of the problem. Consequently, definitive conclusions regarding the utility of the self-concept construct for intervention strategies in a mentally retarded population cannot be drawn. The challenge looms large, and the technology

is at hand; the next step is to directly address the major method-
ological questions. (p. 10)

We agree with Rosenkoetter's assessment to the extent that it is obvious that traditional objective procedures still need to be developed
to measure self-concept in developmentally delayed people. The
same situation exists in reference to other variables critical to a holistic, humanistic philosophy. It is difficult to measure objectively such
constructs as happiness, depression, belongingness, creativity, mutuality, sense of body in space, life-satisfaction, and so on, because
they are complex inferred concepts. We would disagree with Rosenkoetter's statement, however, if it led to the conclusion that such constructs should be ignored, discontinued, or "put on the back burner"
in terms of treatment because of the lack of "objective" measurement.
It is precisely because the issues are so complex—so human—that
they are difficult to measure; and it is precisely because of those same
reasons that they *must* be dealt with to the greatest extent possible in
our treatment approaches. Ignoring the issues does not eliminate
their impact on our clients' lives. Fortunately, however, there *are*
techniques of measurement that are well-grounded in tradition and
in pragmatic reality. Frequently described as "participant observation," this approach utilizes a phenomenological model that seeks to
understand and evaluate the world *from the perspective of the client.*
Participant observation is not a technique that should be thought
of as purely subjective reporting of the "researcher." A dynamic tension must be established between the researcher's role of observer and
participant, by abandoning preconceived or a priori hypotheses (see
Glaser and Strauss, 1967, for a thorough discussion of this issue).
MacLeod (1947) has described this phenomenological approach as
"the adoption of what might be called an attitude of disciplined na-
ivete" (p. 194). Phenomenologists label the suspension of preconcep-
tions as "bracketing." Glaser and Strauss (1967) state that the result of
the traditional objective or quantitative approach is often "a forcing
of data as well as a neglect of relevant concepts and hypotheses that
may emerge" (p. 54). In contrast, Wilson (1977) stresses that phenomenological or "ethnographic research . . . seeks to discover the
meaning structures of the participants in whatever forms they are expressed" (p. 255). He goes on to explain that the research is "multi-
modal" and that the following are all relevant kinds of data:

1. Form and content of participants' verbal interactions
2. Form and content of verbal interactions between researcher and participants
3. Nonverbal behavior of participants
4. Participants' patterns of action and nonaction
5. Traces, archival records, artifacts, documents

Although the seminal work of anthropologist Bronislaw Malinowski (1931) has had widespread impact upon ethnographic-phenomenological studies in anthropology and sociology, the need for phenomenologically oriented studies of persons with developmental delays has been noted by several authors, such as Edgerton (1976), Blatt (1977), Jacobs (1981), and Heshusius (1981). As a field, we have studied relatively little of how the person who is labeled "mentally retarded" or "developmentally delayed" perceives his or her own existence. In fact, we generally have not considered the phenomenological field of the people we serve; nor have we dealt with clients' perceptions of the ecological systems of which they are a part. Indeed, the perceptions of the person with mental retardation have been so neglected that Blatt (1977) stated that no opinions are sought from them since they are "not expected to think" (p. 8).

Phenomenological techniques in themselves may not yield results leading to the reorganization of specific behaviors as would quantitatively oriented designs. However, phenomenologically oriented techniques are not aimed directly at modification of behavior but rather are seen as a prerequisite step. Thus, phenomenal data *may* lead to modification of behaviors based on a clearer understanding of the perceptions of the client — an understanding that was obtained through clearer communication between the "researcher" (participant observer) and the client. In working with developmentally delayed individuals such a process is a critical one that is often missing in our service-delivery systems. A phenomenological approach, however, enhances the profession by providing a clear "set of guidelines to assist the less competent in our care to live their lives in a way most meaningful to them" (Heshusius, 1981, p. 4).

An important aspect of phenomenological-measurement approaches is the valuing of authenticity in the expressions of clients. *Authenticity* may be defined as the accurate expression of meaningful affective material. In a sense authenticity is the cornerstone of phenomenological studies, as objectivity is the cornerstone of quantitative studies. As noted, within the phenomenological, qualitative tradition it is deemed inappropriate for the researcher to impose a priori limitations upon data—a procedure that creates difficulty in perceiving the perspectives of the subject (Broadbeck, 1968). Within this tradition, social scientists hold that one "cannot understand human behavior without understanding the framework within which the subjects interpret their thoughts, feelings and actions" (Wilson, 1977, p. 249).

Within the fields of anthropology and sociology phenomenological designs are employed commonly for research. However, phenomenological approaches have not been limited to social sciences. For example, the entire field of nuclear physics has been imbued with the phenomenological point of view. For physicists "objective reality" does not exist. Rather, the physicist recognizes "reality" as a shared *phenomenon* between the observer and the observed. Participation in the phenomenon can not be avoided by the observer since he is a part of the phenomenon. Zukav sums up the attitude of modern experimental physicists when he states "it is no longer evident whether scientists really discover new things or they create them. Many people believe that discovery is actually an act of creation" (Zukav, 1979, p. 36). And Einstein has written: "Physical concepts are free creations of the human mind, and are not, however it may seem, uniquely determined by the external world" (Einstein & Infeld, 1938, p. 31).

The effectiveness of a phenomenological approach has been evident to us on numerous occasions, through observing the growth of our clients. It is important to realize, however, that even once the relative issues of authenticity and objectivity are resolved, determining *effectiveness* of a technique still remains essentially a question of *values*. A technique is effective only to the extent that it effects changes in something that is valued. We will discuss this issue later in the chapter, but at this point we want to stress again that our *primary* concerns —our most valued goals—are the more abstract internal dynamic ones, such as improving self-concept. However, as pointed out in chapter 1, our creative writing method yields many *secondary* or serendipitous results. Consequently, we have designated *both* a primary and a secondary goal for each activity in chapter 4.

In the remainder of this chapter we describe a variety of methods to measure both primary and secondary goals. Included are methods traditionally associated with the phenomenological, ethnographic, qualitative approach, as well as more empirical, quantitative approaches. We hope a usable balance between the two approaches will be found by the teacher using this creative writing method. From the perspective of advocating treatment that is directed at the whole person, that is delivered in a human, dignified manner, and that is evaluated with reasonable and relevant measues, we now turn to a discussion of those methods.

METHODS OF MEASUREMENT

Methods used to measure can vary according to several dimensions. The techniques discussed below can be utilized from a primarily phenomenological or primarily empirical perspective, with different degrees of objectivity, reliability, and validity (quantitative variables), as well as different degrees of authenticity and therapeutic significance (qualitative variables). The specific target behavior to be measured also will effect the measurement methods chosen. Critical dimensions of measurement include

Individual vs. group measurement
Simplicity vs. complexity of variable (target behavior)
Objective (external) vs. subjective measurement (inferences about internal dynamics)
Standardized vs. nonstandardized instruments
One observer vs. multiple observers
Participant observer vs. nonparticipant observer
Use of clients' self-reports included or excluded
Direct measurement (actual target behavior) vs. indirect measurement (related behavior).

Table 3.1 describes these dimensions.

In each specific situation, decisions as to which of the various dimensions should be utilized must be based on the needs of the students, the teacher, and the agency. Such decisions will dictate the style of measurement (i.e., phenomenological, quantitative, or a combination) and will affect the choice of specific measurement techniques and target behaviors, as well as the ultimate form of the data obtained.

TABLE 3.1   CRITICAL DIMENSIONS OF MEASUREMENT

Individual	*Group*
Data is taken on one person only (e.g., individual intelligence test)	Data is taken on more than one person at a time (e.g., casenotes regarding the whole class)
Simple Variable	*Complex Variable*
Target behavior is clear and distinct (e.g., student comes to class)	Target behavior is amorphous or indistinct (e.g., aggression)
Objective Variable	*Subjective Variable*
Target behavior is external and directly observable (e.g., talking out in class)	Target behavior is inferred from external behavior and is assumed to occur within the person (e.g., self-esteem)
Standardized Instrument	*Nonstandardized Instrument*
Measuring tool has been tested with a sample of the intended population against whose scores the results are compared (e.g., Scholastic Aptitude Test)	Measuring tool that has been designed for the specific population being evaluated (e.g., teacher-designed classroom tests)
One Observer	*Multiple Observers*
Data is taken by one person only (e.g., teacher takes data)	Data is taken by more than one person with results compared or pooled (e.g., teacher and aide take data)

There are many methods of measurement available, some of which will be described here. Sample data sheets for use with these methods are provided in the Appendix. For a thorough discussion and explanation of traditional quantitative forms of measurement techniques, see *Behavior Modification: Principles, Issues, and Applications* (Craighead, Kazdin, & Mahoney, 1976). Wilson (1977) presents a discussion of ethnographic or phenomenological forms of measurement as applied to educational issues.

Casenotes

One of the simplest methods of measurement available is the writing of casenotes. Following work with a given student or students, the

Participant Observer
Data-keeper actively participates in the events or processes being evaluated (e.g., teacher participates in creative writing class and then writes casenotes)

Nonparticipant Observer
Data-keeper does not participate in the process or events being evaluated (e.g., secretary scoring math tests after class)

Self-Reports Included
Students' statements, descriptions, and explanations are included as valid data (e.g., product analysis of students' creative writing)

Self-Reports Excluded
Student's statements, descriptions, and explanations are not included as valid data (e.g., event recording of students' ability to spell words)

Direct Measurement
Target behavior is directly measured (e.g., to measure students' knowledge of similes, the teacher asks them to state the definition of similes — event recording)

Indirect Measurement
Target behavior is indirectly measured by directly measuring another behavior or behaviors that are assumed to be related (e.g., to measure students' knowledge of similes, the students' behaviors in creative writing class are measured through time sampling, event recording, casenotes. Teacher assumes that the students who actually use similes frequently and correctly have a knowledge of similes.)

teacher writes descriptions of the events of the session, in light of the students' needs and past history. Over a period of time trends and changes can be reviewed by reviewing the casenotes. Such trends and changes can then be summarized in narrative statements (e.g., monthly or semiannual summaries). Wilson (1977) points out that within an ethnographic framework narrative summaries, such as casenotes, are not merely "impressions" of what was observed. Rather, the observer must make real efforts to understand the "meaning structures" that determine the person's behavior (p. 253).

Within our creative writing method, casenotes can be utilized by recording basic information about the individual's mood, level of participation, social interactions, facial expressions, body posture, motor acts, apparent affective or cognitive insights, and areas of expressed interests. Additionally, copies of the writings produced in each session should be kept along with the casenotes written. Across time such records can be quite revealing in their longitudinal descriptions of the changes occuring in the students. Casenotes can be particularly valuable in describing relationships and interactions between class members. Particularly in classes where handicapped students have been mainstreamed, casenotes may provide important insights into the attitudes and expectations of class members — and their effects on the handicapped students in the room.

Event Recording

Another form of measurement, somewhat more objective, is event recording, in which the observer (e.g., teacher or therapist) writes down each time a particular event (the "target behavior") occurs. (See figure 1 in the Appendix.) For instance, if the particular concern was to increase a student's self-esteem, one target behavior that could be recorded would be the frequency of positive statements the person makes about himself or herself. Each time such a statement is made, the observer would either write the statement down verbatim, or place a check or other symbol on a data sheet. In creative writing this technique could be utilized easily by noting the positive self-statements made in students' stories about themselves. In such a case, event recording is used to measure *indirectly* one variable (self-esteem) by directly measuring another variable (positive self-statements) that is infered to be related to self-esteem. Assuming that the observer is accurate about the recording of target behaviors and the choice of behaviors that are relevant to the overall goal, event recording is a relatively accurate form of measurement. However, it can be quite cumbersome and time-consuming, particularly if the target behavior occurs frequently. A solution to this problem is called time sampling.

Time Sampling

Time sampling is very similar to event recording, in that the observer writes down the event as it occurs. However, in order to avoid the necessity of having to observe constantly, or recording data incessantly, a schedule is devised that breaks the day or treatment session into small components of time, during which data is taken. For instance, in the example given above, where the goal is to increase self-esteem and the target behavior is positive self-statements, data might be recorded only during the first five minutes or last five minutes of each one-hour treatment period. This would be considered a fixed-interval time-sampling procedure. Other fixed-interval schedules could include: the first minute in each fifteen-minute block of time; every other five-minute block of time; the first, third, fifth, seventh, and ninth minute out of every ten and so on. As mentioned previously, it is essential that the needs and resources of the client and agency be considered in determining what type of data and schedule to use.

RANDOM TIME SAMPLING.   Another form of time sampling is random time sampling where a timer is set to ring or buzz at random intervals such as after one minute, two minutes, seven minutes, two and a half minutes, thirteen minutes, and so forth. Each time the timer rings, the observer records data for a set interval, such as fifteen seconds or one minute. This procedure would have been worked out ahead of time, but the actual timing of observations would be random, thus resulting theoretically in somewhat more objective data. (See figure 2 in the Appendix.) The time-sampling methods are based on traditional quantitative techniques, but even these techniques can be implemented with a phenomenological perspective by choosing target behaviors that are believed to measure internal aspects of the individual. For instance a student's choice of a seat in close proximity to other students could be seen as an indication (or indirect measure) of his or her sense of belonging. Similarly, verbal statements made by the student that are relevant to the topic discussed could be seen as a measure of mutuality.

Product Analysis

Another form of data is product analysis. This can take a variety of forms, but involves actually interpreting, counting, or otherwise evaluating the actual product produced by the client. For instance, if the goal were to increase self-esteem, the target behavior might be to improve the accuracy of the client's self-image, and the method might be participation in drawing classes. The method of product analysis would then be reviewing the drawings of himself or herself that the client produced throughout the course of the class. An objective, standardized scoring procedure could be used (such as the criterion of the Goodenough-Harris Drawing Test, 1963), or a more subjective, clinical interpretation could be made by the instructor. Product analysis can take many other forms, including interpretation of the symbolic content of stories, poems, or other written works; as well as other qualitative assessments of the products a student might produce in other areas of classroom activities. Some common examples of product analysis are the grading of papers by teachers, reviews of the quality of work done on assembly lines by factory-workers, and the final checks of the computer equipment on rocket-ships before take-off. Product analysis is sometimes called trace analysis or artifact analysis and is a traditional phenomenological approach as well as a frequent quantitative approach.

Standardized Tests

There are of course a number of standardized, published tests that have been designed to measure a variety of criteria ranging from intelligence to motor dexterity. It is beyond the scope of this chapter to delineate these; for a discussion of such tests see Aiken (1976). It is essential to remember, however, that the decision to use a standardized test must be made based on the criteria listed earlier in the chapter. There is no magic in standardized tests—they are only useful if they meet *your* needs, and more important, the needs of your students.

Checklists

There are many published surveys and checklists that can be used to measure attitudes, interests, perceptions, beliefs, knowledge, and so on. (See figure 3 in the Appendix.) As for standardized tests, delineation of these is beyond the scope of this chapter. However, numerous journal articles contain this information. Various checklists, surveys, and rating scales can be adapted or designed for specific use with our creative writing method. For instance, again using the example of self-esteem as the overall goal, a checklist might be designed to record a variety of target behaviors believed to be related to self-esteem. Included might be items such as "dresses neatly," "makes positive self-statements," "smiles frequently," "makes positive statements about the future," "approaches work-tasks optimistically," "completes projects begun," and so on. The range and scope of such a checklist is unlimited. There are also a number of persons with whom, or locations in which, the checklist could be used; for example, students' parents or other staff members could be asked to fill out the checklist periodically. In some cases, other students could even be asked to fill out checklists. In schools where peer governments have been established, checklists could be a useful tool. In classes where handicapped students had been mainstreamed, checklists could be particularly useful in revealing the level of acceptance among the class members, especially if they were used over the course of a semester or full year, during which change would probably occur gradually. Checklists can be used by virtually anyone who comes in contact with a person and based on observations in virtually any location. The assumption made in using checklists in creative writing would be that changes revealed by the checklists were related to involvement in creative writing.

Anecdotes

Another form of data that can be requested of virtually anyone who comes in contact with a student is anecdotal information. (See figure 4 in the Appendix.) A format frequently used for anecdotal data is the antecedent-behavior-consequence format (A-B-C) in which the observer is asked to record the target behavior each time it occurs, describing the *antecedent* (what happened before the target behavior), the *behavior* itself, and the *consequence* (what happened after the behavior). The descriptions should be given using brief narrative statements and recording the time and location and other pertinent information. The A-B-C format is useful in helping develop a clear conceptualization of the dynamics occuring around various behaviors, thus clarifying the client's motivations and frequently the motivation or attitudes of significant others in the client's life, as well. The A-B-C format has been used both in phenomenological and quantitative studies. As with checklist data, an assumption made when using anecdotes is that changes described are related to participation in creative writing.

Self-Reports

Finally, a simple but frequently essential form of data is a student's self-reports. Simply asking a student what he or she thinks, feels, desires, believes, and so on can be an extremely revealing and critical form of data. Self-reports are naturally subject to the same questions of interpretation, and of reliability and validity, that the other forms of data are. But they are potentially a rich source of information that should not be overlooked and may provide much more authentic information than otherwise would be available. Additionally, the simple act of asking a student to express himself or herself can be beneficial and therapeutic. This form of data is a naturally occuring one throughout this creative writing method.

CHOOSING GOALS

Todd Risley (1973) has presented what he describes as a difference between experimental significance and therapeutic significance of data. In rigorous scientific study "experimental significance" may be obtained through careful planning, thorough data-analysis, use of complex statistics, and so on. But Risley points out that such experimental significance may or may not be "therapeutically significant." For instance, if a study were designed to measure the frequency of blue-eyed males compared to hazel-eyed males, it is probable that statistical significance, or experimental significance, would be obtained. But unless that information was important to someone, or to society as a whole, therapeutic significance would not be obtained. Similarly, in taking data or designing goals, it is possible to obtain experimental significance without obtaining therapeutic significance. A simple example would be a goal for a student to achieve spelling skills, where the objective was to learn to spell two new words per week. Data could be taken (in this case, event recording) that might indicate that significant progress had been made: the client indeed learned to spell new words. This undoubtedly would be experimentally significant, particularly if the improvement were maintained over a period of time and verified by observations of more than one observer. However, it is possible that such an "improvement" may not be therapeutically significant in and of itself. *More* than the objective data itself would be needed to determine therapeutic significance. For instance, what was the student's feeling about this improvement? Was it a major breakthrough that he or she is proud of, even though it was relatively small in numbers? Did this improvement motivate him or her to work harder and continue to improve? Did it improve self-esteem? Did it enable the agency to justify keeping this program in an overall service-delivery system that helps him or her in other ways? Was the student able to use the new skill in meaningful ways in everyday life? How much time was spent teaching this skill that could have been used in providing other services? There are a variety of ways in which therapeutic significance can be determined. But the basis of such a determination is a *value system*. By nature, values are not objective. Consequently, the ultimate basis of data keeping, goal setting, and measurement and analysis of treatment-success is *not* data, but values. This does not undermine or take away the need to use objective methods of measurement, but it is necessary to maintain a proper perspective regarding goal setting and data keeping. Unless the goals you set and the data you keep assist the student in achieving goals that are valuable to him or her, then the data (no matter how objective or accurate) may be meaningless.

The essence of goal setting should include at least three components. First, the actual current and potential abilities of the individual should be considered. Goals should not be set that are unreasonably difficult or out of range of the student. Second, the value systems of *both* student and agency should be overtly considered. While the values of the agency should be recognized, the value system of the student must take precedence. This is where authenticity (e.g., truly understanding the student's values and perceptions) is so critical. Ideally, all goals should be consistent with the student's values and preferably should also be consistent with the agency's values. Finally, goals should take into account the interplay between the student's history, current life-situation, and future goals. Most important, the *whole* person must be considered, including social, emotional, cognitive, physiological, and cultural aspects.

PERSPECTIVE

In implementing this creative writing method, it is our hope that the goals teachers choose will be therapeutically significant. In most cases the primary goals given in the activities seem to us to be of the most therapeutic significance. If the secondary goals are utilized we hope they will be utilized as indicators (indirect measures) of the primary goals. Ideally a balance will be achieved between primary and secondary goals — a balance that reflects the emphasis of this book on holistic, humanistic education.

CHAPTER 4

Activities

This chapter describes the activities that make up our creative writing method. They are divided into four sections: "A. Starting the Group," "B. First Writing Activities," "C. Intermediate Writing Activities," "D. Advanced Writing Activities." Although our stress is always on the process, with the products (including written pieces as well as learning of specific writing skills) being secondary, the activities do lend themselves to organization in sequential order from basic activities to more complex activities. Thus section A includes activities that allow the group members to get acquainted, establish mutual trust, and begin to express themselves in a "safe" environment. Section B includes activities that increase the students' self-concept, awareness of others in the group, and recognition and expression of feelings, and that provide the initial experiences of writing. Section C includes activities to increase awareness and use of language concepts and to enable abstract expression through imagery and personification. Finally, section D includes more complex activities that facilitate written expression through the use of plot and a variety of written forms such as short stories, poems, songs, and so on.

It will be beneficial for all students to keep a collection of their writings in a personal anthology. This should be made a positive and ongoing aspect of involvement in these activities, and may include illustrations by the students, if they desire. The anthology will assist the teacher in evaluating the students' growth on an ongoing basis and will be a source of pride for each student.

Consistent with our primary concern for process goals, such as facilitation of expression, improvement of self-concept, and establishment of trust between participants, and our secondary concern for learning of specific writing skills, each activity delineates both a primary and a secondary goal. In each case the primary goal relates to the process goals listed above, as well as other interpersonal or intrapersonal goals, such as improved mutual understanding, improved listening skills, values clarification, and development of problem-solving skills. By choice the primary goals are generally more abstract, more dynamic, more complex, and less directly measurable than the secondary goals that deal with specific writing or expressive abilities. As stressed throughout this book, we believe a more holistic, dynamically oriented approach is needed in working with developmentally delayed individuals. Our design of the activities to reflect both primary and secondary goals grew from our efforts to translate a holistic, humanistic philosophy into specific, describable treatment approaches. A second reason for including both kinds of goals in each activity is to provide the teachers who use this book the structure that may be necessary to allow them to implement this method, even in school systems or agencies that require accountability through documentation of increases in specific measurable behaviors. Our hope, however, is that teachers using this method will be faithful to its holistic, process-oriented flavor and will allow the secondary goals to remain *secondary*. The power of this method is in its process orientation. If this is lost by over-emphasizing the secondary goals, then our creative writing method is not truly being implemented. Conversely, by stressing the process goals, especially the overall goal of increasing students' expression, the teacher will find that the students will *want* to learn how to "improve" or clarify their expressions. Thus, the teacher may use the students themselves as a barometer indicating when to move ahead to new and more challenging activities.

Each activity also includes a description of one or more strategies. We envision the descriptions being used as parts of teachers' lesson plans or as parts of students' individual plans written by interdisciplinary teams; consequently we have tried to make each strategy both concise and clear. We have included suggestions for evaluating the success of each strategy. (Although checklists and time-sampling methods are not listed as suggestions for individual activities, they may be appropriate based on the teacher's or individual's needs.) Also included are comments on special uses of each strategy, or problems or other aspects of the strategy to be considered.

Recommendations for the use of each strategy with students of different functioning levels are also provided in each activity. *In general, any student who has expressive verbal skills consisting of at least two- and three-word phrases can participate in this creative writing method, since it is not necessary for the students themselves to actually write down their words.* Certainly, virtually all students within Educable Mentally Retarded (EMR) classrooms or who are mainstreamed in regular classrooms could participate. We have found that many other persons also can participate and benefit, particularly in the more basic activities described in sections A and B. Consideration must be given, however, to the relative heterogeneity of the class, not only during implementation of the creative writing method, but during other class time as well. If the class is normally conducive to participation by varying levels of students, then the creative writing method activities can be implemented with a quite heterogeneous group, each individual participating at his or her own level.

Two final points must be stressed. As we advocate a holistic, integrative view of individual persons, so we advocate a holistic, integrative application of habilitative arts. For example, several activities utilize more than one art form simultaneously. We have found such integrated arts activities to be exceptionally useful and beneficial in our work with developmentally delayed students. We encourage the teacher to be flexible and adaptive enough to use an integrated arts approach, whenever possible. This can be done even when one particular modality (such as creative writing) is the primary activity.

This leads to the last point: *Be flexible.* The activities we describe should *not* be followed rigidly like a computerized formula. The *essence* of this entire book is a recognition of the individual, unique creative potential within every developmentally delayed student. That same potential lies within each teacher. Use it! Let the activities that follow stimulate, challenge, and guide you — let them facilitate your ability to be creative. Be adaptive and flexible in discovering your own ability to facilitate expression by your students. HAVE FUN!

SECTION A. STARTING THE GROUP

This section presents activities to establish trust and encourage freedom of expression and creativity within the group. Creative writing per se is not emphasized at first, although most of the activities can be used successfully in later stages of the group's experience to stimulate writing.

Almost any experience can be used to stimulate creativity as long as it is enjoyed by the participants, makes them feel good about themselves and allows outward expression. In early stages tactile stimulation and kinesthetic experiences are especially useful with handicapped persons in facilitating expression. Even when the handicap is of a physical nature, children should be encouraged to engage in these activities. Kinesthetic activities have been identified as a primary mode of learning and as a way for handicapped people to organize their thoughts and feelings. Movement therapy has taught us that even cognitively impaired individuals can learn kinesthetically through physical memory traces. The tactile and movement activities in this section are also excellent ways to establish trust among group members on a very basic level.

Activity A. 1: Ground Rules

PRIMARY GOAL
To develop a sense of mutual trust and physical and psychological safety in students

SECONDARY GOAL
To enable students to describe the basic ground rules of Creative Writing classes

STRATEGY
1. When creative writing is first introduced to the class, stress that it is time for fun and creativity.
2. Tell the students that they can say *anything* they want during these sessions. Stress that *anything* is OK.
3. Give examples of areas the students may think are taboo based on your knowledge of the specific students. Typical taboo areas are sex, complaining about the teacher, complaining about school, expressing anger, expressing fear, telling someone you love or like them, cursing, and saying nothing.
4. Tell the students there are only a few rules during these sessions:

- Nobody will be allowed to hurt anyone else *physically.* (The teacher will prevent this if necessary.)
- Everyone will be allowed to talk (or to choose not to talk).
- Everyone will be expected to be courteous by listening when others are talking.
- The teacher will "run" class, but the students will have as much input into subject matter as possible (i.e., students have freedom of choice within each activity regarding specific expressive content).

EVALUATION METHOD
Ask students to list out loud the ground rules.
Casenotes.
Anecdotes.

LEVELS OF APPROPRIATENESS
All levels

VARIATIONS
You may want to list the ground rules on the chalkboard or develop another visual aid to help the students remember them. You may also need to repeat these rules periodically until it is clear the students know them.

COMMENTS
It takes most students several sessions or more to believe that they *really* can talk about anything. It is critical that when they do begin to open up, the teacher receive their expressions positively and empathically.

Activity A.2: Reflective Techniques

PRIMARY GOAL
To facilitate expression by students

SECONDARY GOAL
To establish a mutual communication pattern between teacher and

student based on verification and feedback of cognitive and affective expressions

STRATEGY
1. The use of reflective techniques should not be thought of as a separate activity, but one to be used as a natural part of all the activities.
2. The essence of reflective techniques is *empathic communication* (see chapter 2 for discussion). The teacher strives to understand what the students say. The cognitive content as well as the affective content is important. (For example, *Student:* "I never get to go home." *Teacher,* reflecting only the cognitive component of the student's statement: "You haven't been home in a long time." A better reflection would include both cognitive and affective components: "You're very lonely and you want to go home.")
3. The teacher must seek feedback from the student as to whether the teacher's reflections were accurate. In the example above, the teacher would ask the student if the reflection was accurate. The student might respond, "Yes, that's it," or might respond, "No, I'm not lonely at all. I like living with my aunt. I'm glad I don't get to go home, 'cause my parents are mean to me." The teacher could then reflect the statement about the student's parents, and the communication cycle would continue.
4. In teaching creative writing, the teacher needs to develop a sense of timing and a sensitivity to issues that are critical to the students. At some point in the transaction sequence, the teacher should help students structure their expressions by asking that a story or poem be written. This allows students to feel that their expressions and perceptions are valued and accepted. But it also helps the teacher set natural limits based on the level of trust in the class, the other class members' reactions, the time left, and so forth. Students then channel their expressions into writing and have the opportunity to view their own perceptions from a different point of view when hearing them read out loud. This is often an extremely therapeutic, cathartic process for students, as discussed in chapter 2.

EVALUATION METHOD
The teacher must evaluate himself or herself in terms of ability to use reflective techniques. The same process that is applicable to the stu-

dents is applicable to the teacher. For instance, the casenotes or anecdotes written about students can be reviewed by the teacher with the goal of evaluating his or her own involvement in the process. A daily log may also be kept, describing the overall process in the class, enabling the teacher to grow along with her or his students.

LEVELS OF APPROPRIATENESS
Reflective techniques are appropriate at all levels in the classroom and should be used to reflect both verbal and nonverbal communication by students.

Activity A.3: Creating a Sense of Group

PRIMARY GOAL
To develop a sense of mutuality among students

SECONDARY GOAL
To increase the level of trust between group members

STRATEGY
1. Have students sit in a circle where all can see each other.
2. Play soft music, and ask each student to sway rhythmically.
3. Have group members take hands and sway rhythmically together.
4. Be overt: ask students if it was OK to hold "so and so's" hand.
5. Teacher overtly points out, "We have created a group."
6. Have each person say their name. Stress that each one is a member of the group. Tell the class, "We are friends here."
7. Have each person shake hands with each member of the group individually (ritualized).
8. Tell the class, "We are sharing space." To the accompaniment of music, have the class:
   • Breath together rhythmically holding hands
   • Move together rhythmically (simple movements)

EVALUATION METHOD
Casenotes
Anecdotes

LEVELS OF APPROPRIATENESS
All levels. With higher-functioning students, the teacher may allow more opportunity for students to verbalize their feelings.

VARIATIONS
Students may be paired off together and asked to synchronize their breathing or movements while listening to music. Have students describe their feelings if possible.

COMMENTS
These exercises must not be thought of as empty ritual. The teacher's overt discussion of the individuals *becoming a group* is critical. The concept of group should be stressed to the students frequently through creative writing activities.

Activity A.4: Gross Motor Activities for Group Consciousness

PRIMARY GOAL
To develop a sense of mutuality among students

SECONDARY GOAL
To increase the level of physical contact between students

STRATEGY
1. Have students sit or stand in a circle.
2. Engage the class in some basic breathing and movement activities as described in activity A.3.
3. Ask one member of the group to enter the center of the circle and make some simple movements.
4. Ask the other students to imitate or "try on" the student's movements.
5. Encourage students to comment on how the movements feel. Ask them to consider how breathing feels, how the legs feel, the arms, and so forth.
6. Give each student an opportunity to enter the center of the circle.

EVALUATION METHOD
Casenotes
Anecdotes

LEVELS OF APPROPRIATENESS
All levels

VARIATIONS
The students can "mirror" one another, after pairing off in twos. This helps establish *each* individual as an important part of the class, assuring that no one is left out.

COMMENTS
Many students initially may be defensive or timid about engaging in gross motor activities. It is important that the teacher become involved in these activities. This will tend to minimize the students' resistance or hesitancy to engage in movements. It will also help the teacher assist the students in interpreting and describing the movements of others. The teacher must be careful to be aware of each student's special sensitivities and needs.

Activity A.5: Noise vs. Music

PRIMARY GOAL
To increase sensory awareness in auditory area

SECONDARY GOAL
To enable students to differentiate between music and noise

STRATEGY
1. Prepare some cassette tapes with recordings of music, alternating with recordings of noises, such as honking horns, doors slamming, dishes breaking, wood scraping, chalk scratching, paper fluttering, a noisy cafeteria, and machines running. The music selections should be varied, including lyrical classical music as well as jazz, rock, popular, and atonal music.
2. Have the students listen to the recordings and tell you whether they think the recordings are music or noise.
3. Point out that music is organized, structured, rhythmical, melodious, and harmonious (usually). Point out that some students tapped their feet, clapped their hands, or danced to the music selections.
4. Ask students to try to dance or keep rhythm to noise recordings, pointing out how hard that is.
5. Ask students how listening to music versus listening to noise makes

them feel, or what they think of when they listen to the music or to the noise.

6. Ask the students to listen very carefully to the sounds of the room with no recordings playing. After about thirty seconds, ask them to describe what they heard.

EVALUATION METHOD
Event recording: record whether students can correctly identify obvious music recordings from obvious noise recordings. Record whether students can imitate or create varying rhythm.
Casenotes.

LEVELS OF APPROPRIATENESS
All levels

VARIATIONS
Use sound-effects record. Allow the students to experiment making different noises with available material. Ask the students to try to make rhythmic noise and nonrhythmic noise. (Demonstrate if necessary to get the concepts across.)

COMMENTS
This activity can be a good precursor to a music period or to writing about how different music makes students feel. It can also be effective in getting across the idea of mood as created by music.

Activity A.6: Music to Create a Mood

PRIMARY GOAL
To stimulate expression

SECONDARY GOAL
To help students integrate auditory, visual, and kinesthetic sensory input

STRATEGY
1. Carefully select music to be played for the students. Find music in which the mood is obvious — joyful, sad, action filled, or angry.
2. Tell the students you have selected music just for them. All you want is for them to listen to it. (The length of listening time for the

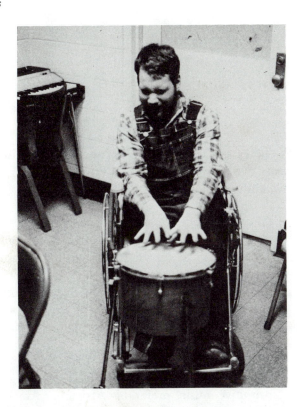

Music and movement are critical as integral parts of the creative writing milieu. The integration of art forms allows the whole person to be involved in expression.

students should be based on the teacher's estimation of their attention span.)

3. Ask each student how the music made them feel. Ask them what kind of imagery or mental picture they saw in their minds. Give each class member a turn. (See Comments.)

4. Ask each student to either draw a picture of what they "saw" and/or do a dance to the piece of music (the student who chooses to dance will more than likely begin to tell a story about the dance).

EVALUATION METHOD

Event recording: ask students to identify obvious moods in the music, recording successful attempts.

Product analysis: review the students' drawings in light of the known theme of the music.

Casenotes.
Anecdotes.

LEVELS OF APPROPRIATENESS
All levels

VARIATIONS
Variations are endless since a wide variety of music can be utilized and since this activity can be used frequently as the students progress in their expressive ability.

COMMENTS
Using music to create a mood and facilitate expression is one of the most basic methods we use. It can be integrated into almost every other activity in this book. The music does not always have to be discussed with the class. It can simply serve as a mood setter at the beginning of the session or throughout as a backdrop to other activities.

The following list of music to elicit creative responses should help a teacher get started in this activity.

Rhythmic
Any style of primitive music, preferably African or American Indian.
Most students can relate to these cultures since they have had wide exposure in the media.
Strauss waltzes: the waltzes are usually highly rhythmic, have a calming effect, and can also help when exploring happy moods.
Chinese Shantung music (on Nonsuch label): the music of the Shantung Chinese is both rhythmic and foreign sounding enough to create a response.
Peruvian mountain music: extremely lyrical and rhythmic, also with a foreign sound that will create a response.

Calming Music
The Afternoon of a Faun, by Debussy.
Chopin waltzes.
Piano pieces by Satie.

Sad Music
Adagio from *Swan Lake*, by Tchaikovsky.

Funérailles, by Liszt.

Many of the Chopin études.

"Addio del passato," by Verdi (*La Traviata*). Opera can be used effectively because many students relate more easily to the voice. Being in a foreign language also is an advantage because the emotion will come through without the words coloring the response of the student.

Happy Music

"La Bouf sur la toit," by Darius Milhaud.

Selections from *The Threepenny Opera*, by Kurt Weill.

An American in Paris (selected sections), *Porgy and Bess* (selected sections), and various instrumental versions of other music by Gershwin.

Peter and the Wolf, by Prokofiev.

Exciting Music

Overture to *La Forza del destino*, by Verdi.

Overture to *West Side Story*, by Bernstein.

Mazeppa Symphony, by Liszt.

Overture to the motion picture *Jaws*.

"The Ride of the Valkyries," by Wagner.

First Violin Concerto, by Sibelius.

Indian ragas.

Angry Music

"The Seventh Trumpet," by Donald Erb.

The Rites of Spring, by Stravinsky (selections).

Mephisto Waltz, by Liszt.

Selections from Jimi Hendrix albums.

Selections from *Elektra*, by Richard Strauss.

Ninth Symphony, by Mahler (selections).

Activity A.7: Foot Painting

PRIMARY GOAL

To increase students' self-concepts, in the area of awareness of their physical selves (e.g., body size, proportion, balance)

SECONDARY GOAL
To use gross motor art activities to facilitate students' descriptive expressions

STRATEGY
1. Bring in large pieces of cardboard and several colors of finger paint.
2. Play music that is fairly rhythmical, such as marching-band music.
3. Tell the students, "We are going to march to the music and make a painting."
4. Have the students take off their shoes and socks and roll up their pants (make sure you have told the students ahead of time to wear old clothes this day).
5. Pour rather large quantities of finger paint onto the cardboard and have the students march rhythmically to the music, walking through the finger paint and leaving footprints on the cardboard. Have them walk back and forth, in circles, make their "initials," and so forth.
6. It may be necessary to have only one or two students at a time on the cardboard, depending on class size. However, it is better if most or all the students participate simultaneously, in order to emphasize the group aspect of this activity.
7. While the students are foot-painting, or immediately after, ask them how it felt. Ask them what the music made them think of; how the other students looked as they were foot-painting; what the picture reminds them of; what the colors make them think of.
8. Point out that the *group* has made a picture and talk about cooperation and sensitivity to one another. Be sure to be upbeat and positive.
9. Have the group each generate a comment or two about the experience and incorporate all the students' remarks into a narrative story or poem about the activity. Read it to the class.

EVALUATION METHOD
Casenotes
Anecdotes

LEVELS OF APPROPRIATENESS
All levels. With physically handicapped students, the teacher may need to assist directly or have the students help one another. Most students can have at least one footprint or handprint placed on the card-

board as their contribution. *Don't do the activity if someone has to be left out completely.*

VARIATIONS
Make cardboard murals of handprints or fingerprints (this is good if there are many physically handicapped students). The students can also stand or sit around a table and work on long sheets of paper, making free-form paintings with finger paint or tempera, while listening to various types of music. Higher-functioning students or classes experienced with other phases of creative writing could be asked to incorporate the mood and style of the music into their painting (e.g., "What color do you think of when you hear that music?").

COMMENTS
This is an excellent activity to integrate with the group-consciousness activities, as well as with tactile and kinesthetic activities described earlier. It helps increase students' self-image, develop a sense of group identity and mutual trust, and stimulate much verbal expression naturally. The teacher may also use it to emphasize affective language on a basic and nonthreatening level (e.g., "The paint felt squushy, and I felt silly and happy stomping around").

Activity A.8: Art Activities for Fine Motor

PRIMARY GOAL
To develop increased sensory awareness

SECONDARY GOAL
To increase students' abilities to participate in and describe various fine-motor stimuli

STRATEGY
1. Have students participate in a variety of arts activities utilizing fine-motor skills. Activities such as finger painting, making collages, or cutting out mobiles are all appropriate.
2. Ask students to describe the sensations involved, encouraging both positive and negative descriptions. *Make a point of letting the students know their descriptions are valid* (i.e., there are no right or wrong answers).

3. Allow the students to experiment, when possible, in attempting new activities. Also allow the students as much choice as possible, eliciting their descriptions of reasons for their preferences.
4. Give students positive feedback about the results of their artwork. Remember that the primary emphasis is *not* on the artwork, but on the students' sensory awareness and descriptive efforts.

EVALUATION METHOD
Casenotes
Anecdotes

LEVELS OF APPROPRIATENESS
All levels

VARIATIONS
Many different fine-motor activities can be utilized. This activity can be integrated with efforts to enhance the sense of group by having the students engage in mutual fine-motor activities (such as two students finger painting on one piece of paper) or by having students imitate various fine-motor activities initiated by other students.

COMMENTS
The concept of integrating art activities is repeated frequently throughout this book. Integrating art forms is an excellent means of stimulating expression among students and is particularly helpful in allowing a person to become completely engaged in the activity.

Activity A.9: Texture Bag

PRIMARY GOAL
To develop increased sensory awareness in tactile areas

SECONDARY GOAL
To enable students to recognize differences in various textures and to identify them by name

STRATEGY
1. Bring in a variety of textured materials, such as scouring pads,

feather dusters, washcloths, powder-puffs, rocks, sand, smooth synthetic fabric, leaves, sticks, sea shells, buttons, cardboard, packing material (the inflated "bubbly" kind that pops when you squeeze it), styrofoam peanuts (another packing material), toy blocks, and so on.

2. Put ten or twelve very different objects in a paper bag, without letting the students see them (make sure you have several *more* objects than students).
3. With students seated in a circle, tell them that you are going to play "Texture Bag." Pass the bag around the group, and ask each student to pick out the *smoothest* item, *without looking at them*. Have each student pick an object.
4. While they are choosing an object, talk to them about different textures, using basic descriptive words such as rough, smooth, soft, hard, bumpy, sticky, fuzzy. Ask each person to explore the objects with their fingers to discover which ones are which.
5. Remind them occasionally which texture they are looking for (smooth).
6. Encourage spontaneous expressions, both verbal and nonverbal (i.e., facial expressions or body movement), of how the students react to each object, using basic reflective techniques.
7. After each student has picked an object, have the class pass all the objects around the circle and explore each one comparing tactually and visually. After everyone has explored each item, ask each student to say which one they think is smoothest.

EVALUATION METHOD
Casenotes: narrative summary.
Periodically ask students to identify textured objects you present to them and record number identified correctly.

LEVELS OF APPROPRIATENESS
All levels; especially appropriate at the lower levels or as an early warmup activity for higher-functioning students.

VARIATIONS
Ask for different texture to be chosen. This activity can also be used with objects of different size or shape. It can be used in conjunction with activity A.10.

COMMENTS

If the class is one where a variety of arts activities are encouraged, this activity can be a very natural lead-in to a period of sculpting (using materials brought in to create forms and textures), making collages, making mobiles, making wind chimes, and so forth. When class is ready for writing, this activity can be used to stimulate descriptions or stories (e.g., "The softest thing I ever felt was . . . ," or "I don't like sticky things because . . .").

Activity A.10: What Is It?

PRIMARY GOAL

To develop increased sensory awareness in tactile areas

SECONDARY GOAL

To be able to recognize differences in various tactile stimuli (i.e., shape, size, texture, temperature) in order to identify objects by name

STRATEGY

1. Bring in a variety of common objects (pen, pencil, rubber ball, pebbles, paper, chalk, soap, rice).
2. Place one at a time in a bag or box, and ask each student to feel it without looking at it and guess what it is.
3. Ask them to describe what the object feels like.
4. Give other students a turn, asking them to explain why they agree or disagree with previous guesses.
5. Reveal the object and point out essential features (e.g., size, shape).
6. Repeat, varying the objects.

EVALUATION METHOD

Event recording: record students correct responses to a variety of objects presented.

LEVELS OF APPROPRIATENESS

All levels

VARIATIONS

Have one student feel the object and describe it while the other students guess what it is. For large objects, use a blindfold, letting one or two students try while the others observe, and give hints until a correct guess is made. Have students bring in objects they think will stump the class (a good introduction to the concept of mystery and problem solving).

COMMENTS
This activity can be used in conjunction with other tactile activities. It can serve as a lead-in to writing stories about the kind of object (e.g., "I like to play ball because. . . .") or about "mysteries" or problems the students have faced. The activity can be used to stimulate drawing or painting of the objects and writing of stories while painting.

Activity A.11: Temperature

PRIMARY GOAL
To develop increased sensory awareness

SECONDARY GOAL
To be able to recognize gross differences in temperature

STRATEGY
1. Bring in a variety of objects of different temperatures (e.g., glasses of water, ranging from very cold to very warm).
2. Ask students to feel the objects and identify the coldest or warmest.
3. Give feedback about their response pointing out the differences between cold, cool, warm, and hot.
4. As the objects you brought in near room temperature, have the students feel them again, pointing out that temperatures change.
5. Have the students explore the room with their hands, looking for objects of different temperatures (e.g., windows may be cold, a radiator hot). Students should be encouraged to describe the temperature of what they feel.
6. Encourage students to touch each others' hands or faces, and point out that some people feel cold, some hot, and so forth. Ask each student how they feel.

EVALUATION METHOD
Event recording: Record students' responses to presentation of objects of different temperatures.

LEVELS OF APPROPRIATENESS
All, best for lower levels or as warm-up for higher levels (especially those who may not ordinarily touch one another). Can be done outdoors.

COMMENTS
This technique can facilitate social interaction and touch in a nonthreatening way. It can be used to stimulate stories about how students feel about being touched. This activity is also a good way to introduce the concept of uniqueness of each person.

Activity A.12: Smell

PRIMARY GOAL
To develop increased sensory awareness in the olfactory area (smell)

SECONDARY GOAL
To be able to recognize different common smells

STRATEGY
1. Bring in a variety of liquids with distinct odors, such as lemon juice, vinegar, perfume, salt water, Coca-Cola, rotten eggs, alcohol, cleaning fluid, gasoline.
2. Soak small cotton balls in the various liquids and have the students smell them and try to identify the liquid.
3. Encourage expression regarding the smells such as pleasant, unpleasant, sour, bitter, sweet.
4. Ask the students what the smells remind them of.
5. Have the students look through a selection of magazines with pictures of foods and other common household items (e.g., ammonia, cleaning fluids, bleach) and try to identify pictures of items they have smelled.
6. A collage could be made of different items that smell alike, or a variety of different smelling objects.

EVALUATION METHOD
Event recording: record students' responses to a variety of different odors.

LEVELS OF APPROPRIATENESS
All levels

VARIATIONS
Use items of different tastes.

COMMENTS
At higher levels this activity can be especially useful in stimulating stories about past experiences associated with different smells (e.g., "In the spring I always used to enjoy going home and helping my father mow the grass, but the smell always made me sneeze!").

Activity A.13: Visual Stimuli

PRIMARY GOAL
To increase sensory awareness in the visual area

SECONDARY GOAL
To improve students' abilities to discriminate and describe various visual stimuli

STRATEGY
1. Ask each student to look around the room and choose an object to describe to the class.
2. Tell the students *not* to name the object.
3. Giving each student a turn, ask each one to answer simple questions such as "Is the object big or little?" "Is it red? Green? Yellow?" "Is it light or dark?" "Does it look heavy or light?" "What does it do?"
4. As the student answers the questions, have the class try to figure out what the object is, with the teacher providing logical guidance (e.g., "It can't be the chalkboard because Johnny said it's yellow — and the chalkboard isn't yellow").
5. Encourage the class to look around the room trying to find the object, calling out their guesses. The first student to guess gets to describe his or her object next.
6. Remember, the object of this activity at this point is not the students' descriptive ability, but their *visual searching* and sensitivity.

The teacher should aid verbally as much as possible, but get the students to look as much as possible.

EVALUATION METHOD
Event recording: note which students are able to guess objects.
Record narrative summaries of the general response of students to this activity, noting the kinds of objects they pick and their ability to discriminate and describe small details of objects.

LEVELS OF APPROPRIATENESS
All levels

VARIATIONS
Play "What Is It?" (activity A.10), having all students look at an object and take turns describing it to a blindfolded student who has to guess what it is. Bring flashlights to class, and have students "paint pictures" on a darkened ceiling with their flashlights while other students watch and guess what is "painted." Utilize naturally occurring opportunities to point out visual details in materials brought into the classroom or special events that occur during the day. Encourage the students to look for and describe things they see throughout the day. This could be combined with a "show and tell" activity or with a variety of other art activities, such as painting, sculpting, or photography.

COMMENTS
Good visual discrimination and subsequent descriptive ability are essential prerequisites to successful expressive language when imagery is introduced.

SECTION B. FIRST WRITING ACTIVITIES

The techniques in this section have been used primarily to stimulate initial interest in use of words. The emphasis is mainly on sentence structure, word usage, and the basic concept of telling a story, rather than on complete works.

The various games, activities, and projects that follow have been used successfully to stimulate creative writing among our students. We encourage the reader to apply the principles discussed earlier in this book to create more techniques; the possibilities are almost limitless.

Activity B.1: If I Were

PRIMARY GOAL
To increase students' self-concepts in the area of identification of desired or valued roles

SECONDARY GOAL
To increase students' abilities to tell a story about what famous person they would like to be

STRATEGY
1. Ask students to name some of their favorite television shows.
2. Ask them each to name some of their favorite characters, and then have each student choose *one* character about whom to write a story.
3. Ask the students to think about why they like or don't like the character. Talk with the class about the things the person does, especially how he or she treats other people, and the adventures that he or she has on the show.
4. Working with each student individually, have them each make up a short story about their character. The teacher may get them started by using a complete-the-sentence procedure (e.g., Teacher: "J. R. Ewing got up one morning and told his mom [Miss Elly] that . . . ").
5. Most students will at least be able to complete one sentence started by the teacher. If they are not able to continue at that point, the teacher may ask general probing questions, such as "What happened next?" "What did _____ say?" "How did that happen?"
6. It is likely that some students will tell very long stories without any assistance needed from the teacher. In such cases, it may be necessary to point out that this assignment is for short stories and that the class will be able to write long stories another time. Remind them that everyone must get a chance, and that time must be saved to read the stories to the class.

EVALUATION METHOD
Casenotes
Product analysis

LEVELS OF APPROPRIATENESS
All levels

VARIATIONS
The teacher may start the discussion by asking each class member to complete a sentence beginning with "If I were _____, I would. . . ." The teacher should choose the character, being sure it is someone the class knows. Television characters can be used, but so can popular heroes such as astronauts, sports figures, local celebrities, or well-known politicians. Personal characters known to the class or to the individuals can also be used especially as the class matures and grows in mutual trust. Students can write about what they would do if they were a relative or special friend, or another class member — or even if they were the teacher. Once the students have completed the first sentence, have them write a story, using the same technique described above under strategy.

COMMENTS
This activity may be used effectively with activities B.10 and B.15, emphasizing use of the students' imagination, identifying their own values, and identifying and describing affective aspects of the characters about whom they are writing.

Activity B.2: Being Big and Being Small

PRIMARY GOAL
To increase awareness of self-image in the area of body size

SECONDARY GOAL
To facilitate verbal descriptions of one's own body

STRATEGY
1. Have a small group of students stand in a circle, and ask them to breathe in deeply and exhale. Demonstrate as necessary. Encourage the students to take deep breaths and feel the air entering their bodies.

2. Tell the class that when you breathe in deeply you feel VERY BIG. Demonstrate by extending your arms out to your sides in large sweeping movements—as you inhale. This should be done slowly and exaggerated for emphasis. Ask the students to try to imitate you.
3. Tell the class that when you exhale you feel very small. Close your body up with inward sweeping gestures, until your hands and arms are held tightly against your chest, with your shoulders curved in toward your chest. Encourage the class to imitate you.
4. Repeat the above in-out procedure several times, continuing to exaggerate for emphasis and encouraging the class to do the same. If necessary, go around the circle giving individual assistance to each student, using gentle physical guidance of their bodies through the activity. Point out to the students any areas of their bodies that feel particularly stiff or tense.
5. Ask the students how "being big" feels. Ask them how "being small" feels.
6. Tell the class to relax and either sit down in a circle on the floor or return to their normal seats in class. Ask each student how being big and being small felt. Have them repeat the in-out sequence in their seats if necessary.
7. Record each response made by each student, even if only one word. Once everyone has finished describing their feelings, tell the class, "We have written a story—let me read it to you." Order the responses so that all the "being small" comments are read first, then all the "being big."
8. Emphasize what a good job the class did, and tell them how excited you are that the class created a story. Remind them that they will have a chance to write stories in the future, both as a class and individually.

EVALUATION METHOD
Simple casenotes describing each students' verbal and nonverbal responses
Product analysis of each individual's comments

LEVELS OF APPROPRIATENESS
This is a basic activity that is best used at the earliest stages of creative writing or as a very simple warm-up later on. With higher-functioning students or with an "experienced" writing group this activity is

best used when combined with other art modalities, such as dance, pantomime, or drama.

VARIATIONS

This can be used with other art modalities, such as dance or drama. Other body movements can be tried ranging from simple acts such as walking around the room, to jogging, hopping, and so forth. More complex (and more symbolic) activities can be attempted; for example, using their bodies to imitate objects such as trees, buildings, birds, or airplanes. Virtually any movements that they can imitate or create themselves are appropriate to stimulate verbal expression as long as the movements help them to become better aware of their bodies.

COMMENTS

It is critical that activities at this level are fun and nonthreatening to the students. Using their bodies to stimulate expression is a good way to start because they are naturally familiar with how their bodies feel (at least partially) and will probably have described some feelings in the past. However, the teacher must be very careful not to allow this exercise to become threatening to students who may be very sensitive and/or guilty about their bodies. It is essential to keep the activity pleasant, lighthearted, upbeat, and fast paced and to let the students provide cues to you as to when to move on, speed the pace, take a break, and so on.

Activity B.3: Lying Down and Tracing

PRIMARY GOAL

To increase awareness of self-image in the area of body proportion

SECONDARY GOAL

To facilitate verbal descriptions of one's self

STRATEGY

1. Bring in large pieces of cardboard like those used in refrigerator boxes. (Pieces must be large enough for the tallest student to lie down on.)
2. Divide the class into groups of twos, and have each student take turns tracing the body of the other student who lies down on a large

piece of cardboard. Heavy duty felt-tip markers or crayons should be used. You may choose to prepare or sensitize the class to this exercise by having them trace small parts of each others' bodies, such as hands, feet, or arms.

3. Point out interesting features of the various drawings as they are made (e.g., "Look at John's drawing—see how long his arms are!" or "Wow! Sarah's picture looks like she's dancing").
4. When everyone has been drawn, have each student describe his or her picture to the class. Accept whatever level verbal description each student is capable of. Tell each student that he is creating a story about himself. Encourage students to actually make up a story, as well as to describe themselves. If they have trouble doing this, ask them to tell the class what they did today, or tell about some recent special event. Record each person's statements, and praise whatever efforts are made.
5. When each student is finished, read back each story. Be careful not to compare stories or praise some stories while ignoring or passing over others; treat each student equally.

EVALUATION METHOD
Simple casenotes
Product analysis

LEVELS OF APPROPRIATENESS
This is appropriate at any level, assuming the students' physical ability to make the tracings.

VARIATIONS
Students can paint or color in their tracings as a graphic arts activity, as teacher works his or her way around the room writing down each student's story as the paintings are made. Using the tracing or painting as a starting point, a pictorial representation of important parts of the students' day can be made. Students can draw small pictures around the perimeter of their body representing basic daily activities (e.g., picture of student at breakfast, on school bus, in school, going home, going to bed). Instead of drawing, students can look through magazines and find pictures to cut and paste down, representing their daily activities. These pictures then can help guide them in telling a story about their day. (Once the pictures are in front of them, in sequence

around their body tracing, the students may find it easier to recount events in a story-like fashion.)

COMMENTS
This activity is almost always a favorite of students and generates many descriptive comments naturally. At higher levels or with experienced classes this activity can be used to introduce or reinforce the concept of plot (i.e., temporal sequence) when used in conjunction with drawing or pasting down pictures of the days' events. This is also an excellent source of information about events in the lives of students that may be important or difficult to them, but otherwise unknown to the teacher (e.g., a student who reports that he or she "never eats breakfast because my mom doesn't get up").

Activity B.4: Nature Walk

PRIMARY GOAL
To increase general expressive ability

SECONDARY GOAL
To increase students' abilities to tell a story about things in the environment

STRATEGY
1. Take the class on a nature walk. Tell each class member to look for three objects to bring back to the classroom.
2. Point out objects in the environment that are familiar to most students (e.g., sticks, rocks, trees, birds, houses, sky). Describe aspects of such objects, such as shape, size, color, location, and so forth.
3. Point out unfamiliar items in the environment or items that the students may frequently overlook (e.g., moss on trees, birds' nests, shed skins of snakes, pinecones, fallen leaves of many different shapes and colors). Describe these objects as in step 2.
4. Have students select their three objects and bring them back to the classroom.
5. Ask each student to describe the nature walk. Tell them to talk about such things as what they liked best, what they didn't like,

what they saw that they were afraid to touch, what they touched that hurt or that felt good, and what they chose to bring back to class — and why.

6. Ask students to make a collage of found objects as a group project and then write a group story about the collage and the day's events. (Group story should be written using the technique described in activity B.2.)

EVALUATION METHOD
Simple casenotes
Product analysis (of stories)

LEVELS OF APPROPRIATENESS
This activity is appropriate for all levels that are capable of walking around outside as a group.

VARIATIONS
This activity can be built around a theme or a particular holiday season, such as Halloween or Christmas.

COMMENTS
Much serendipitous learning about a variety of subjects can occur from this activity (e.g., safety rules of outdoor travel, knowledge of various plants and wildlife, awareness of seasonal changes).

Activity B.5: Animal Game

PRIMARY GOAL
To increase self-concept, in the area of identification of likes and dislikes

SECONDARY GOAL
To increase students' abilities to tell stories about animals in the environment

STRATEGY
1. Ask students to identify various animals. For some classes it will be necessary to show pictures of animals for identification.

2. Ask students how the animals sound: cow, moo; cat, meow; and so forth.
3. Ask each student to select an animal to pretend to be.
4. Have students act out movements and sounds of the animals. Have each person tell a story about the animal he or she acts out.
5. Break into groups, and have each group form their own play with dialogue and action.
6. Have each group perform their play for the class, while you write down dialogue and action (or tape record).

EVALUATION METHOD
Product analysis
Casenotes

LEVELS OF APPROPRIATENESS
All levels, depending on complexity of task (see variations)

VARIATIONS
A range of complexity is appropriate utilizing this basic format. The key elements are the use of the students' imagination and their choosing animals they prefer to identify with. Simply choosing an animal from a variety of pictures and making up a short story or simple poem is adequate at beginning levels or with low-functioning persons. A group story is also appropriate in such cases with each person completing a sentence, such as: "I like _____ because. . . ." At advanced levels, this activity can generate skits or short plays, complete with music and props, to be used as class performances. This is particularly appropriate around holidays or theme days like fall festival or spring festival. In such cases the "Animal Game" could be used as a springboard to help the class participate in creating their own production rather than simply learning a more standard production by rote.

COMMENTS
Although the same format of looking at pictures and choosing an object with whom the student identifies is repeated in later activities, the "Animal Game" is significant because of the ease with which many students are able to identify with animals. Most students are already familiar with this basic concept, thus simplifying the activity. It is also

less threatening than identifying with other human figures (as in later activities). "Animal Game" is really the reverse of reading fairy tales —instead of hearing a ready-made story and identifying with the characters or animals, the students identify with animals first and then produce their own "fairy tale."

Activity B.6: Magazine-Pictures Game

PRIMARY GOAL
To increase students' sensitivities to the feelings of others

SECONDARY GOAL
To increase students' abilities to identify and describe the feelings of others

STRATEGY
1. Bring in pictures from magazines or newspapers, showing people in a variety of emotional states: elated, dejected, frightened, bored, happy, sad, angry.
2. Put all the pictures on a table, and have the students walk around the table looking at each picture. Once they have all had a chance to study each picture, have them sit down, while the teacher puts all the pictures into one pile.
3. Hold up one picture at a time and ask the class to identify the emotion. If there is disagreement among class members, facilitate a discussion. *It is not necessary to get consensus* at this point. However, if the entire class is obviously not familiar with the descriptive terms for the person's emotion, the teacher may provide input.
4. Based on the discussion in step 3, ask the students to write individual or group stories about what they think caused the person to feel the chosen emotion. Particularly when the class is not able to reach consensus about the emotion, stories should be generated justifying the position taken.

EVALUATION METHOD
Casenotes
Anecdotes
Event recording (of ability to identify emotional states)

LEVELS OF APPROPRIATENESS
All levels

VARIATIONS
The students can be asked to look through magazines or newspapers trying to find a variety of pictures showing a particular type of emotional state. The class could discuss all the pictures and reach a consensus about the "best" angry picture, the "best" bored picture, and so forth. Collages of pictures could be made by the class, or a "picture of the month" could be selected to be posted in the classroom. The teacher may also elaborate on the basic concept of identifying emotions in others by asking students to identify and imitate the various emotional expressions of other students in the room. This should only be done after the class is well integrated as a group and a high level of trust and mutual respect exists. At this point, however, the concept of role playing one another may be very beneficial, both in increasing students' understanding of themselves and each other and in stimulating expressive stories. The teacher may allow students to take turns

Many modes of art stimulation evoke the mental imagery that emerges in creative writing.

occasionally being "Teacher for a Day" (or "Teacher for an Hour") running the class and acting as the teacher does. This can be a real eye-opener for both the teacher (who should take the part of a student) and the students.

COMMENTS

This is an excellent activity to integrate with self-concept activities. Remember the emphasis at this stage is primarily to help students learn to identify emotions in others. It is fairly nonthreatening to do this from pictures of strangers. The teacher will want to stress to the class that *all* feelings are OK and that everyone has feelings. Eventually the class may begin identifying emotions in other class members and themselves. This activity may also be utilized as part of a problem-solving activity (e.g., "How do you solve the problem of *feeling* angry at someone, but not being allowed to express that feeling by hitting or hurting the other person?").

Activity B.7: Feeling Responses Through Pictures

PRIMARY GOAL

To increase students' abilities to identify and express their own emotions

SECONDARY GOAL

To increase students' abilities to identify and describe emotional expressions of others

STRATEGY

1. Show the class a picture that displays social action between two people or animals.
2. Discuss the picture with the class.
3. Have each student pretend he or she is one person or animal in the picture and respond verbally to the situation (e.g., "John, you pretend you are the little boy in the picture. What are you saying? Why?").
4. Let each student have a turn. Record their responses. Do not comment on the content they create. Merely reinforce the fact that they participated.

EVALUATION METHOD
Event recording (e.g., pretest and posttest of "correct" identification
    of various prejudged pictures
Casenotes
Anecdotes

LEVELS OF APPROPRIATENESS
Best with higher-functioning students, but should not be automati-
cally eliminated with lower-functioning students. This is very appropriate for a heterogeneous group or a class where developmentally
delayed students are mainstreamed, because the students learn from
one another.

VARIATIONS
This activity can be repeated many times by varying the pictures; by
using the same pictures periodically with the students and comparing
the differences in responses by each individual student as well as by
the class as a whole. There are also a variety of marketed products
available for affective education of handicapped students that may be
useful in conjunction with this activity.

COMMENTS
The ability to identify and express emotions in oneself and in others is
critical to one's own mental health, as well as to one's ability to participate in creative writing in a truly meaningful manner. Consequently
we stress affective expression throughout virtually *all* creative writing
activities. Though we have included several examples designed specifically to enhance this skill, it is critical that the concept of affective
expression be integrated with most of the other creative writing activities, particularly those in section C and section D.

Activity B.8: Comparisons

PRIMARY GOAL
To improve students' general expressive ability

SECONDARY GOAL
To develop the basic concept of opposite (or antonyms) in students

STRATEGY
1. Introduce to the class words such as large, small, pretty, ugly for comparative usage involving two objects.
2. Encourage the class to initiate their own opposite word usage in describing objects of their choice.
3. Ask the class to illustrate the comparative qualities that were discussed.
4. Ask the students to write a story using the appropriate descriptions learned.

EVALUATION METHOD
Event recording (of students' abilities to generate a pair of opposite descriptors for various objects)
Casenotes

LEVELS OF APPROPRIATENESS
Most appropriate at higher-functioning levels. With lower-functioning students this concept can be approached through informal feedback during other activities that provide "natural" (and more concrete) examples. For instance, the teacher might call a student's attention to the difference between a very *big* painting or sculpture and a very *little* one done by another student. If the basic difference between big and little is grasped by the student, the teacher might point out that big is the *opposite* of little (e.g., "Sarah's picture is *very big*. It's the *opposite* of Sam's. His is *very little*").

VARIATIONS
A variety of opposite pairs is possible and a list could be made of all the opposite-pairs words the class has thought of. As the class levels off or plateaus in their ability to think of new opposite pairs, a game could be made of seeing who can remember more opposites. Other art activities could be combined with the class list by asking students to draw pictures or make paintings or sculptures to illustrate the various opposite concepts. As they do so, each student could make up a story or poem, or the class could make one up as a whole.

COMMENTS
This is a good way to stretch the students' expressive abilities, while keeping the task relatively structured and simple. (Once the concept

of opposite is understood, it is often easier to ask a student, "What is the opposite of . . . ?" than to ask, "How else could we describe . . . ?" or "What else can you think of to say about . . . ?")

Activity B.9: Problem Solving

PRIMARY GOAL
To increase students' sense of independence

SECONDARY GOAL
To improve students' problem-solving skills

STRATEGY
1. Bring in several pictures showing antisocial or antagonistic interaction between two or more people. Newspaper, magazines, and comic books are all good sources for such pictures.
2. Show the class a picture (starting with a fairly simple and non-threatening one, such as baseball player arguing with an umpire) and facilitate a discussion among the class about what is happening in the picture.
3. Be sure that the class identifies the basic critical elements of the picture (i.e., who, what, when). If the members of the class are not able to do this, the teacher should point out the critical elements.
4. Once the basic elements have been identified, ask the class what they think caused or started the incident.
5. Have each individual or the class as a whole make up a story about the picture, about a similar incident that happened to them, or about what they think they would do in such a situation. In making up the story, have students respond to questions such as: How could the situation have been avoided? How could the situation be avoided the next time? What steps were necessary to solve the problem?

EVALUATION METHOD
Casenotes
Anecdotes
Product analysis

LEVELS OF APPROPRIATENESS
Most appropriate at higher levels. Use concrete examples in class to

get concepts across to lower-functioning students. (For example: wait until someone actually has a fight or argument; then discuss with entire class what could have been done to avoid it. Stories can be written about the real event by the individuals or the class as a whole, but don't use writing stories as a punishment.)

VARIATIONS
Variations are endless based upon pictures you bring in or situations that arise in class. As with the "Animal Game" (activity B.5), a skit or play can be based on this activity.

COMMENTS
This is a good activity to integrate with affective-expression concepts. (For instance, "If the problem is that Johnny is *angry*, how could he solve this problem? Could he show his anger in some way other than hitting Natasha? How? Can we write a story about this?") The overall issue of *problem solving* is often neglected as a skill to teach developmentally delayed people. One of the best ways to enhance problem-solving skills is to allow people to work out problems that occur *naturally* in their lives and to experience the consequences. Unfortunately this may often be considered impossible or too risky. Exercises such as this one allow a reasonable alternative to facilitate learning of problem-solving skills.

Activity B.10: The Magic Land Writing Game

PRIMARY GOAL
To facilitate students' abilities to use imagination

SECONDARY GOAL
To increase students' abilities to tell a story about their own fantasies

STRATEGY
1. Ask each student to close his or her eyes and listen to a "make-believe" question (e.g., "You are in a land far, far away. A magic make-believe land. You have a magic wand that can do anything you want it to do. Tell me about the wand. What will you do with your wand?").

2. Record the stories as each child begins to speak. Where possible the student should keep his or her eyes closed.
3. Background music that is conducive to the activity may also be used.

EVALUATION METHOD
Casenotes
Anecdotes
Product analysis

LEVELS OF APPROPRIATENESS
Higher-functioning students or heterogeneous groups.

VARIATIONS
Variations based on the students' imaginations are endless. To stimulate this activity, the teacher can use virtually any props (e.g., visual aids, verbal cues, music, other art forms, previous class experiences, holidays).

COMMENTS
Although this activity is primarily for higher-functioning students, don't make the mistake of *assuming* that your lower-functioning students do not have active imaginations. In many cases the evident lack of imagination is merely the result of lack of expressive ability, cognitive *organization*, and/or the lack of opportunity to express and someone willing to listen. Some of the most beautiful expressions we have witnessed have come through the imaginative processes of severely retarded persons.

Activity B.11: Which Came First?

PRIMARY GOAL
To increase general expressive ability

SECONDARY GOAL
To develop or increase the concept of sequential occurrences

STRATEGY
1. Ask the class to listen carefully, then slowly state the names of three familiar animals.

2. Ask the class which one you named first. Second. Third.
3. Name three additional animals and repeat step 2.
4. Repeat step 3 several more times.
5. When the students have grasped the concept of basic sequence, ask them to listen carefully again as you tell a very short story about *one* animal, giving *three* distinct action phases (e.g., "A bear *slept all winter*, then *ate strawberries all spring*, then *played in the woods all summer*").
6. Ask the class to tell you what happened first. Second. Third.
7. Repeat with a different story.
8. Ask the class members each to make up their own simple stories involving three actions.

EVALUATION METHOD
Product analysis
Anecdotes

LEVELS OF APPROPRIATENESS
All levels. If lower-functioning students are not able to repeat the orders cited, they should still benefit from their efforts to listen carefully and attend. They will probably grasp the basic concept of plot or sequence, and most verbal students can at least identify which came *first* or *last*, if not the total proper order.

VARIATIONS
Many other objects, themes, and actions can be used, based on a teacher's imagination. Actual class experiences can be used. The class can be asked to make a group mural, depicting the sequential order of a class event.

COMMENTS
This is a basic introduction to the concept of plot. At higher levels it may be appropriate to introduce the word *plot* and discuss its importance in stories (see plot activities in section D).

Activity B.12: The Mystery Prize

PRIMARY GOAL
To increase students' abilities to use imagination

SECONDARY GOAL
To increase students' abilities to tell a story about their imaginative thoughts

STRATEGY
1. In front of the class, place wrapped boxes of various sizes, in which there are prizes. Make sure that the prizes can be used in the class-room. Vary the style of the packaging. Some should be wrapped with ornate wrapping paper, some with newspaper, and one in a sealed paper bag. Be sure there is a box for each student.
2. Ask each student to guess what is in one of the boxes.
3. Ask each student to tell a story about the mystery prize.
4. After the stories are complete, let the class open the boxes.

EVALUATION METHOD
Casenotes
Anecdotes
Product analysis

LEVELS OF APPROPRIATENESS
Virtually all levels, depending on complexity of task (best with classes generally experienced with creative writing)

VARIATIONS
Verbally describe packages rather than bringing in real ones. Use this activity in combination with "If I Were," activity B.1.

COMMENTS
With higher functioning students, this activity can be used to intro-duce the concept of mystery and elaborate the concept of plot.

Activity B.13: Famous Paintings

PRIMARY GOAL
To increase student's awareness of their own feelings (moods)

SECONDARY GOAL
To enable students to write stories illustrating the concept of mood

STRATEGY

1. Bring into class a variety of famous reproductions illustrating various overt moods. Show these paintings to the class.
2. Help the class identify the mood of each painting.
3. Discuss how the mood was created (i.e., color, content, shapes).
4. Ask how the class thinks the artist was feeling when he or she painted this painting.
5. Ask if the students have ever felt this way.
6. The writing task can now be structured around either a story coming out of the visual experience of the painting or a story about the students' experiences involving the emotion illustrated in the painting.
7. Use music that is related to the mood of the painting to reinforce the concept, but do not comment on it.

EVALUATION METHOD
Casenotes
Anecdotes
Product analysis

LEVELS OF APPROPRIATENESS
All levels, once basic familiarity with creative writing has been achieved

VARIATIONS
Have students paint their own paintings in conjunction with this activity. Students can then look at each other's paintings and try to determine the feelings of the painters.

COMMENTS
Paintings should be selected carefully so they establish and maintain students' interest.

Activity B.14: Combined Visual Art and Writing Activities

PRIMARY GOAL
To increase students' general expressive abilities

SECONDARY GOAL
To improve students' concepts of mood

STRATEGY

1. After the students have become familiar with various reproductions the teacher has shown in class, have the class paint pictures depicting the same emotion.
2. Discuss the importance of color to create mood.
3. If the task is structured so that everyone is working on the same emotion in their paintings, have music that reinforces this mood playing in the classroom.
4. Do not comment on the content of the painting, but point out the best color usage to create a particular mood. (If for any reason the class cannot mix the proper colors, the teacher should have them prepared in advance, in this way structuring the appropriate response.)
5. When the paintings are completed, have the class begin writing a story about the paintings, combining art and writing activities.
6. Encourage the students to describe the colors in terms of their stories. (If students have been introduced to the concept of imagery, reinforce the concept of "painting with words.")

EVALUATION METHOD
Casenotes
Anecdotes
Product analysis

LEVELS OF APPROPRIATENESS
All levels

VARIATIONS
Many variations are possible based on the paintings brought into class and the students' imaginations.

COMMENTS
The story that a student may tell may have nothing to do with the *content* of a painting. Do *not* tell the student there is a discrepancy between what he or she says and what is in the painting. *The painting is the springboard for the creative response.* (Only if the *mood* of the piece radically changes from, let us say, a happy mood to a sad mood should you comment. Much depends on the developmental and functioning level of the student. In early stages of development it is com-

mon for children to swing their mood responses radically. However, for children where this typically constant shifting of affective response is integral to their disability, the teacher must positively restructure the situation for elicitation of the most appropriate response.)

Activity B.15: Puppetry as a Motivation for Creative Responses

PRIMARY GOAL
To increase students' general expressive ability

SECONDARY GOAL
To increase students' awareness of basic aspects of stories: character, plot, theme

STRATEGY
1. Have the class make hand puppets (from papier-mâché or from socks). Ask the students to choose an emotion to be displayed on the face of the puppet: happy, sad, angry.
2. Spontaneous play with the puppets could produce some good verbalization to be recorded by the teacher. (For example, *Teacher:* "Hello. Who are you?" *Student:* [Response]. *Teacher:* "Where do you live?")
3. If the structure is present, a spontaneous puppet show will emerge from small groups. The dialogue should be recorded on tape and transcribed.
4. Help the students to design a structured show based on their spontaneous play. This is an excellent way to teach the concepts of character, plot, and theme.
   - Character: Each "make believe" person in the play
   - Plot: What happens in the play to the characters
   - Theme: What the play is about (With younger or low-functioning students, it may be easiest to explain *theme* as "what we learn from the play.")
5. The dialogue as it emerges should be written or taped and read back to the class as a written document of a joint creative writing venture.
6. Music should be selected by the teacher (or with participation of

the students where possible) to enhance the theme and music of the
puppet play.

EVALUATION METHOD
Casenotes
Anecdotes
Product analysis

LEVELS OF APPROPRIATENESS
All levels. The secondary goal is most appropriate with higher-functioning students.

VARIATIONS
Many variations depending on teacher's and students' imaginations.

COMMENTS
Puppetry can be a strong motivator to instill a creative response from
students. A carefully structured puppet project can involve all the arts
modalities. Children enjoy the process of making puppets, which involves body image and affect. The goal can be extended to involve
students in the production of a puppet show including kinesthetic and
musical elements.

SECTION C. INTERMEDIATE WRITING ACTIVITIES

These activities are used to enable a student to create integrated,
complete products with knowledge and use of grammar, imagery,
and other specific writing skills. The emphasis is always on creativity,
and the student is not criticized for using incorrect grammar or spelling; however, the techniques facilitate learning through a natural
process, with feedback given in a positive manner.

It often happens that students do use incorrect English while writing creatively. The teacher should not correct grammar in the early
phases of the project. It will only have the effect of creating frustration and negative experience.

If the grammar is so poor that the student's point of view is lost completely, the teacher should sit with the student on a one-to-one basis

and very kindly ask if there is not another way to make the same statement. Together teacher and student can explore the possibilities. A happy compromise is usually found. If the student refuses to change what he or she has written, leave it at that. But the next time give a similar assignment and remediate the problem while the student is writing. Only when the student has enough confidence in his or her own work (which is a reflection of teacher attitude), may you begin teaching formal rules of grammar.

Spelling will not be a problem if the creative writing is done by dictation. However, there may be situations when both student and teacher will want the assignment written by the student. If that is the case, do *not* correct spelling. The assignment was for self-expression.

Activity C. 1: Introduction to Imagery

PRIMARY GOAL
To help students expand their imaginations

SECONDARY GOAL
To develop a basic understanding of the concept of imagery

STRATEGY
1. Read a selected story or poem to the class.
2. Lead the class in a discussion of the content of the story.
3. Treat the content of the story like a painting or motion picture or television show. Ask the class if they "saw" the characters or objects. What did they look like? What did they do?
4. Ask specific questions relating to the piece read. (For example, "What color was the hat?" "How big was the bird?") Go back to the writing to point out the correct answer.

EVALUATION METHOD
Casenotes
Anecdotes

LEVELS OF APPROPRIATENESS
Best with higher functioning students or with heterogeneous groups

VARIATIONS
Once the concept of imagery is grasped by students, the teacher should build upon their ability to use it in their creative writing. Imagery potentially can be utilized with almost every other writing activity in this book.

COMMENTS
Imagery is one of the most important elements of writing that can be taught to the students. Properly understood it will teach young people to expand their imagination. It will also enable students to generalize this concept to other areas of cognitive growth, bringing with it a richness of detail that is often lacking in young or developmentally delayed people. Furthermore, imagery is the basis of all literature and especially poetry. It is most often imagery that brings a piece to life on the page and allows it to live on in the memory. Within the context of this book, imagery will also mean richness of detail in prose that will individualize a character, object, or concept. You may define *imagery* to your students as follows: "Imagery is what we call painting a picture in your mind. You can see the picture in your mind just by hearing or seeing the words."

Activity C.2: Painting with Words

PRIMARY GOAL
To expand students' abilities to use their imaginations

SECONDARY GOAL
To develop in students the concept that imagery is like "painting with words"

STRATEGY
1. Write on the chalkboard the word *house* (or any simple noun).
2. Ask the class to tell you about this house. What does it look like?
3. Ask the class to close their eyes and see a house in their minds. Ask each student what he or she saw. You will receive many kinds of answers (e.g., "It was big." "It was red"). Each answer should be rewarded. Tell the class they are painting with words.
4. Have each student pick an object of his or her own choice. Once the students have made their choice ask them to paint the picture

with words. If they have trouble picking an object, you may give them a list from which to choose. If they should say they don't know what the object looks like, give them a list of adjectives from which to choose (e.g., big, small, large, tiny, red, blue, old). When each student gives his or her response, reinforce the answer with praise. There should be no wrong answers. Often the answer may appear inappropriate, depending upon developmental level. For instance, suppose a student is to attach a description to the word *car*. Instead the student says, "My father's car." The educator's response to the student should not be negative, but should be something like, "Good. Can you tell us what your father's car looks like? Can you paint a picture of it with words?" When the student answers with a color or a shape, respond positively. Tell the student he or she has just painted a picture with words.

EVALUATION METHOD
Casenotes
Anecdotes
Product analysis

LEVELS OF APPROPRIATENESS
Best with higher functioning students or with heterogeneous groups

VARIATIONS
Use a variety of stimuli to elicit descriptions, such as magazines, objects in the room, objects outside, other artforms, and so on. The students can also be asked to expand their paintings with words into stories, poems, or plays.

COMMENTS
The idea of painting with words has been extremely useful in getting across the concept of imagery to our students.

Activity C.3: Painting Pictures with Words

PRIMARY GOAL
To expand students' abilities to describe their own imaginative concepts

SECONDARY GOAL
To increase students' abilities to use imagery, with emphasis on detailed descriptions of objects

STRATEGY
1. Each student should think of an object in his or her mind.
2. Have one student tell the class the object chosen.
3. Then each student in turn should imagine that object and "describe" it adding a detail that was not mentioned before.
4. When no one can think of another descriptor or when the class begins to get confused or forget what others have said, go on to another student and a new object.
5. Reinforce throughout that the class is "painting a picture with words."

EVALUATION METHOD
Casenotes
Anecdotes

LEVELS OF APPROPRIATENESS
Best with higher-functioning students or heterogeneous groups

VARIATIONS
Students can pick one object and then make up individual stories or a group story about it. The following sequence could easily lead to a story about haunted houses: *Person 1:* "I see a house." *Person 2:* "The house is red." *Person 3:* "The red house is spooky." *Person 4:* "The spooky red house has spiderwebs in the windows." The class or individuals can draw, paint, or sculpt objects as described by the other students.

COMMENTS
Although this activity is called a "game," as are many of the other activities in this book, it is important that they don't turn into formalized competition. The game-like quality of these activities is a reflection of emphasis on fun and on giving everyone a chance to participate. They should not become games in the sense of winning and losing or "I can do better than. . . ."

Activity C.4: Painting a Picture with Words Together

PRIMARY GOAL
To expand students' abilities to describe their own imaginative concepts

SECONDARY GOAL
To increase students' abilities to use imagery, with emphasis on detailed description of objects and on building on the imaginations of others

STRATEGY
1. Name a noun. As an example, say, "Everybody close their eyes and listen very carefully to the word I will say. In my mind I see a *house*. Now everybody keep their eyes closed and paint a picture of a house in their minds."
2. Ask each student to describe the house he or she imagined. Either write down each response or use a tape recorder. The responses are usually quite varied since a student is forced to draw from his or her own experience. There will be times when the student will repeat exactly what the preceding student has said. The instructor should respond by saying, "Good, you saw the same picture as Joe." Ask the student if she saw something different from the picture Joe saw. Use a word that the preceding student did not use. Let us say he saw a yellow house. Ask if it was an old or a new yellow house. When the student responds, tell her it is not the same picture as Joe saw. She has her very own mind picture. She painted with words her own imagery. Tell her she is an excellent word painter, in that way reinforcing independent and creative thinking.

EVALUATION METHOD
Casenotes
Anecdotes
Product analysis (of the class' production)

LEVELS OF APPROPRIATENESS
Best with higher functioning students or with heterogeneous groups

VARIATIONS
Many variations are possible based on the teacher's and students' imaginations. A variety of materials from the classroom or from outside the classroom can be used to "start the ball rolling."

COMMENTS
Activities that lead to group productions and rely on mutual listening and creating serve to increase group trust, group identity, social skills of students, and general level of expressivity.

Activity C.5: Describing Each Other

PRIMARY GOAL
To expand students' abilities to describe their own imaginative concepts

SECONDARY GOAL
To increase students' abilities to use imagery, with emphasis on detailed descriptions of persons

Group experiences often facilitate creativity, as well as allow relationships to flourish. Groups may be conducted in formal settings such as classrooms or more informally—and spontaneously—in other settings, such as the movement room shown here.

STRATEGY
1. Ask students to sit in a circle.
2. Ask each student to describe the student opposite him.
3. Encourage full descriptions.

EVALUATION METHOD
Casenotes
Anecdotes
Product analysis

LEVELS OF APPROPRIATENESS
Best with higher-functioning students or with heterogeneous groups

VARIATIONS
The variations on the painting with words games (activities C.2–C.5) are endless. The classroom teacher should use a variety of these descriptive games, suited specifically to the class.

COMMENTS
The teacher should be sensitive to the students' individual strengths and weaknesses, and enter into this activity cautiously. It is necessary to structure the activity so that students do not insult, embarrass, or hurt each others' feelings. This can be done by encouraging the students to describe things about one another that they like or that they wish they had. It may also be necessary to keep a very active pace, with a fair amount of teacher-input, so that a sensitive or damaging area can be diverted by the teacher's comments, if necessary. As the group matures in trust and objectivity, it will be possible to allow much more freedom and openness of mutual description in activities such as this one.

Activity C.6: Introduction to Parts of Speech

PRIMARY GOAL
To expand students' abilities to describe their own imaginative concepts

SECONDARY GOAL
To increase students' abilities to use imagery, with emphasis on use of nouns

STRATEGY

1. When the students are familiar with the word games, reintroduce the word *imagery*. "Imagery is what we call painting a picture in your mind. You can see the picture in your mind just by hearing or reading the words. This is called imagery." Give examples by reading poetry.

2. Introduce the concept of the *noun*, and explain it as the object, person, or place they are "seeing" in their minds. Continue, "Words that are people, places, or things are *nouns*. Nouns are very important words. Nouns tell us what some person or some place or some thing *is*. Our names are nouns. The names of things are nouns, [and so forth]."

3. Lead the class in the following activities:
   - Have students make a list of all nouns they see in the room.
   - Have them make two lists: people and things.
   - Then three lists: people, things, and animals.
   - Tell the class: "List all the animals you can think of at the zoo," or "List all the objects in your bedroom," or "List all the people you love," or "List all the people you like," or "List all the emotions you can think of."

EVALUATION METHOD

Casenotes

Event recording (of recognition of nouns from a list, of ability to make a list of nouns, and so forth)

LEVELS OF APPROPRIATENESS

All levels

VARIATIONS

See "Comments."

COMMENTS

There are many varieties of games that can be used to identify nouns. Most special education students learn this rather quickly. The concept of nouns is important because it will help later when students begin creative writing. They will know that all sentences have nouns and this will be an aid for improvement of language clarity. Very often developmentally delayed students will use sentences such as, "It was very big. It was yellow and big." Reminding students beforehand to use nouns helps to make the actual creative experience more positive for them. Then the teacher does not have to ask a question like, "What was yellow and big?" which often adds to the frustration of a student who already has communication difficulties.

Activity C.7: Concept—Adjective and Adverb

PRIMARY GOAL
To expand students' abilities to describe their own imaginative concepts

SECONDARY GOAL
To increase students' abilities to use imagery, with emphasis on use of adjectives and adverbs

STRATEGY
1. After the students have gained an understanding of nouns and they refer to mental pictures as imagery, introduce the concept of adjectives and adverbs.
2. Play "Painting Pictures with Words" (activity C.3). This time when they use a word describing a noun, you respond to them, "Excellent, you told me what _____ looked like. You used an *adjective*. Adjectives name the words that tell me what things look like. These are adjectives."
3. Introduce adverbs in the same way.

EVALUATION METHOD
Casenotes
Event recording

LEVELS OF APPROPRIATENESS
All levels

VARIATIONS
Integrate this activity with other classroom activities or with other art forms. Students should be asked to describe objects or actions they have observed or in which they have participated.

COMMENTS

Although we have included an activity for verbs, stressing a verb seems not as important as the parts of speech above in terms of creative writing because most students in telling a story will naturally stress verbs. Seldom are verbs left out of sentences in the story, possibly because so many handicapped children receive tension release from kinesthetic action. They appear more prone to leave out nouns, adjectives, and adverbs when relating a tale. Typical kinds of sentences might be: "I ran," or "He took it." No other parts of speech are used to provide further explanation.

Activity C.8: Verb Game

PRIMARY GOAL

To expand students' abilities to describe their own experiences

SECONDARY GOAL

To increase students' abilities to express themselves, with emphasis on the use of verbs

STRATEGY

1. Remind the students of the concept of imagery and briefly review or repeat "Introduction to Parts of Speech" (activity C.6), reminding them that nouns are the names of things.
2. Tell them that *verbs* are the words we use to tell what we *do*.
3. Ask each student what he or she is doing right now (e.g., sitting, breathing, listening).
4. Ask each student what he or she did last night or this morning.
5. Ask each student to describe what another student in this room is doing.
6. Identify the verbs the students used in steps 4 and 5, and ask the class to generate a list of verbs by brainstorming as you write on the board. Correct any words that are stated that are not verbs.

EVALUATION METHOD

Casenotes

Event recording (of recognition of verbs from a list, of ability to make a list of verbs, and so forth)

LEVELS OF APPROPRIATENESS
All levels

VARIATIONS
Have students look through magazines, newspapers, and so forth, cutting out pictures of actions and describing them, using verbs. A collage could be made.

Activity C.9: Adjective Game

PRIMARY GOAL
To expand students' abilities to describe their own imaginative concepts

SECONDARY GOAL
To increase students' abilities to use imagery with emphasis on use of adjectives

STRATEGY
1. Introduce words such as pretty, beautiful, lovely, big, large, huge, little, small, and tiny to illustrate the flexibility of descriptive language:
2. Show items that can be described by more than one adjective. Encourage creative usage of the description.
3. Ask students to write descriptions of an object of their choice. (For example, "The flower is lovely, beautiful, gorgeous, marvelous. I love it.")
4. Have the students expand the descriptions into a group story or individual stories.

EVALUATION METHOD
Casenotes
Event recording
Product analysis

LEVELS OF APPROPRIATENESS
All levels

VARIATIONS
Many variations are possible based on the teacher's choice of stimulus words. Other activities in the classroom can be used to stimulate the use of adjectives.

COMMENTS
This activity can be combined with any of the other parts-of-speech activities in this section. It is rare that special stress needs to be put on verbs. (See "Comments" in activity C.7.)

Activity C.10: Adverb Game

PRIMARY GOAL
To expand students' abilities to describe their own imaginative concepts

SECONDARY GOAL
To increase students' abilities to use imagery with emphasis on use of adverbs

STRATEGY
1. Ask each student to state an action (verb).
2. Ask the students to describe actions.
3. Write a list of adverbs (based on the students' responses in step 2) for the students to refer to.
4. Proceed as in "Adjective Game" (activity C.9). Have the class generate a verb-and-noun combination (e.g., "The boy runs"). Then ask: "How does the boy run?" Tell the class: "In your mind picture the boy running." Ask individuals what they imagined (e.g., "The boy runs slowly" or "The boy runs quickly"). Point out individuality of response to illustrate that several answers are possible.
5. Define *adverb* as "a word that describes a verb."
6. Have the class generate individual or group stories.

EVALUATION METHOD
Casenotes
Event recording
Product analysis

LEVELS OF APPROPRIATENESS
All levels

VARIATIONS
Any activity the class engages in can be used to stimulate the use of adverbs. If the teacher has access to the necessary equipment, the class can be videotaped. Students then can watch each other and describe what they see. The teacher can point out the difference between verbs, adverbs, adjectives, and so on. Many other stimulating experiences are possible within the normal classroom context.

COMMENTS
The concept of adverbs is somewhat more difficult than adjectives for some students. In such cases it may be helpful to have students act out the sequence they are trying to describe, while the teacher points out the difference between how the student is *behaving* (e.g., dancing *quickly*, singing *loudly*, screaming *crazily*) and how the person looks (e.g., the *fast*, *loud*, *crazy* boy).

Activity C.11: Personification

PRIMARY GOAL
To expand students' abilities to describe objects

SECONDARY GOAL
To increase students' abilities to use personification in describing objects in the environment

STRATEGY
1. Teacher shows pictures of six inanimate objects. The teacher should take care in choosing these objects; they should be items known to be of interest to the members of the class.
2. Ask students individually to pick the item they like best or that interests them the most.
3. Ask them to close their eyes and pretend that they are one of the objects.
4. One at a time ask students to "show" the class how the object works.

Encourage the students to move and make sounds that the object might make in operation.

5. Ask each student to draw a picture of the object doing whatever it does.
6. Ask each student how it feels to be the object.
7. Ask each student to tell a story about the object from the point of view of the object.

EVALUATION METHOD
Casenotes
Event recording
Anecdotes
Product analysis

LEVELS OF APPROPRIATENESS
Best with higher-functioning students or in heterogeneous groups

VARIATIONS
Teacher can bring in many varieties of pictures, often of subjects that are being taught in other class periods (e.g., astronomy, plant-life, road-hazards). Various works of art can also be used, especially paintings.

COMMENTS
Personification is a standard element of literature. It is a process in which many children naturally engage in the course of their play. The teacher of special education may capitalize on this quality of "play" to create an environment in which creativity may flourish.

Activity C.12: Using Simile

PRIMARY GOAL
To expand students' abilities to describe objects or concepts

SECONDARY GOAL
To increase students' abilities to use imagery with emphasis on use of similes

STRATEGY
1. Read the class examples of poetry that illustrate simple uses of sim-

ile. Tell them that a *simile* is a comparison of two words to each other.

2. Show pictures of two different objects or the objects themselves that share a similar quality. (For example, a green leaf and green ball. *Teacher:* "Here is a green leaf. Here is a green ball. What color is the leaf?" *Student:* "The leaf is green." *Teacher:* "What is as green as a leaf?" *Student:* "The ball is as green as a leaf." *Teacher:* "What else do you know is as green as a leaf?" *Student:* "My bike is as green as a leaf. [Any response is acceptable.]"

3. Students then add endings to various sentences:
   "I am as large as _____."
   "The tree is as big as _____."
   "An ant is as small as _____."
   "The sky is as blue as _____."

4. Ask the students to create similes of their own.

5. Encourage them to incorporate similes into their writing. "When we write, we can use similes to create better imagery."

6. Read the students poems with similes. Ask students to identify the similes.

7. Repeat the definition of *simile*.

8. Have the students write individual or group stories, stressing the use of similes.

EVALUATION METHOD
Casenotes
Event recording
Product analysis

LEVELS OF APPROPRIATENESS
Best with higher-functioning students or in heterogeneous groups

VARIATIONS
Bring in magazines, photographs, objects from outdoors, or common household objects, and use them to stimulate the students' comparisons.

COMMENTS
As with adverbs, this concept is somewhat more difficult for students to grasp. Acting out a situation may help to elicit similes. Emotional, "real life" situations that are still fresh on students' minds work best. (For example, a student acts out argument with father. *Teacher:*

"How did you feel?" *Student:* "I was mad!" *Teacher:* "How mad?" *Student:* "I was as mad as a wild cowboy!" *Teacher:* "Boy, that's mad. That's also a *simile*. You compared yourself to a wild cowboy.") See also activity C.13.

Activity C.13: Similes and Affective Responses

PRIMARY GOAL
To expand students' abilities to describe their emotions

SECONDARY GOAL
To increase students' abilities to use similes in describing emotions

STRATEGY
1. Read to the class, poems that use similes as an effective statement.
2. Ask the class to complete statements such as:
    "I feel as happy as _____."
    "I feel as sad as _____."
    "I feel as angry as _____."
    "I feel as confused as _____."
    "I feel as surprised as _____."
    "I feel as worried as _____."
    "I feel as sorry as _____."
3. Ask students to write a short story or poem using a simile on how they feel today or how they felt in any situation of their choice.

EVALUATION METHOD
Casenotes
Event recording
Anecdotes
Product analysis

LEVELS OF APPROPRIATENESS
Best with higher-functioning students or in heterogeneous groups

VARIATIONS
Have the students act out the feelings they are describing. This can be done individually or with several students. The short "role plays" can

be expanded to skits or plays for the class's use or for presentation to others.

COMMENTS
The use of similes to describe affect is important in creative writing because it gives the students' writing a style and universality that usually did not exist without this skill. Even if the students do not master this skill, they usually benefit from participating in the effort to describe emotions that are meaningful to them, especially if they have the chance to act them out in the "safe" creative writing environment.

Activity C.14: Several Ways to Create a Mood

PRIMARY GOAL
To expand students' abilities to describe emotions, particularly the concept of mood

SECONDARY GOAL
To increase students' abilities to use effective language in describing their emotions, especially moods

STRATEGY
1. Talk with students about their feelings. Try to generate a fairly open discussion. (The feelings divulged may be somewhat shallow, but sincere nonetheless, depending on the level of trust in the group.)
2. Clarify mislabeled feelings if it is clear that a student is using the wrong word to describe a feeling.
3. Ask the class, "How do creative artists express feelings?" To help the class answer, show paintings illustrating various moods, play music illustrating various moods, and/or discuss or demonstrate movement or dance illustrating various moods.
4. Have the class generate individual or group stories illustrative of various moods.

EVALUATION METHOD
Casenotes
Anecdotes
Product analysis

LEVELS OF APPROPRIATENESS
All levels. (Depending on functioning level and age of students, emphasis should vary. Young children tend to move more readily to movement or dance stimuli. Older persons and higher-functioning persons will respond more readily to the more verbal stimuli.)

VARIATIONS
Teachers should gradually develop a file of pictures and a collection of music to use to stimulate activities such as this one. Those resources can then be used to stimulate students' responses.

COMMENTS
Both music and color evoke moods naturally (e.g., red evokes anger or excitement, as does loud, boisterous music). Both music and color (through painting, crayoning) can be used simultaneously with the teacher's verbal input to help students experience moods by doing (through art) and expressing verbally. When using integrated arts activities, the teacher should emphasize the mood that is evoked and should encourage the students to get across their moods in their writing.

Activity C.15: Children Designing Their Own Readers

PRIMARY GOAL
To enhance students' sense of accomplishment and self-esteem

SECONDARY GOAL
To enable students to create their own readers

STRATEGY
1. Explain to the students that you would like them to make up their own stories for reading.
2. Write on chalkboard the words that must be included in the story (they may not know the words yet, but learning new vocabulary may be integrated with this activity).
3. Let students decide what the story will be about; you write it down.
4. You may need to remind students of the words that must be includ-

ed in the story. Usually the story will be written around these words.

5. After the story has been written, have it typed on a primer type-writer.
6. Make one copy for each child.
7. Leave enough room for students to make their own illustrations as part of the activity.

EVALUATION METHOD
Event recording (of students use and knowledge of the listed words)
Product analysis

LEVELS OF APPROPRIATENESS
This is best with students who have some reading skills, however limited.

VARIATIONS
Students can make up stories without the teacher providing stimulus-words. The teacher may help the students choose alternate words that will be easier to read later. The teacher may have the students improvise or act out a short skit, using their own words. This should be tape-recorded and then made into a reader with the students' own words, exactly as on the recording. This may help keep their interest and motivation longer than many other reading activities. Learning to recognize the words will be facilitated through the students' ownership and familiarity with the material.

COMMENTS
A known problem within the special education classroom is often finding appropriate readers for the handicapped child. Most special educators will agree that many readers for handicapped children are not age appropriate and/or not of a high-interest quality to meet the special needs (individual needs) of these children. With a familiarity with creative writing, reading groups and individual children can design their own reading materials. Although the emphasis of this activity is on integrating creative writing with reading skills, the teacher should remember that the creative writing experience itself should continue to be process-oriented and not become a "chore" for students as reading classes sometimes become.

SECTION D. ADVANCED WRITING ACTIVITIES

These activities are designed to help students integrate their knowledge of writing skills into stories or poems that express significant aspects of the writers' perceptions of the world. As in the earlier activities, the stress is on the students' enjoyment of the process, rather than the products produced or skills attained. However, by the time students have begun to participate in activities in this section, they will most likely *want* to make their writing clear and accurate in describing their feelings and perceptions.

Activity D.1: Television Shows: Introduction to Plot

PRIMARY GOAL
To develop students' abilities to express themselves in an organized fashion

SECONDARY GOAL
To increase students' abilities to recognize and discuss plot in stories

STRATEGY
1. Ask students to repeat a story from their favorite television show.
2. These verbalizations should be recorded and used as television reports and included in their creative writing anthology.
3. If there is confusion about sequence of events in telling the story, the teacher does not comment at this point but takes note of which students are having trouble with this.
4. For those students it may be necessary to simplify the exercises in the following way:
   - Stress sequence in stories that are a normal part of classroom language arts.
   - Make lists of events that take place in the classroom.
   - During locomotor activities stress and point out sequence of movements.
   - While playing music, point out which comes first, loud or soft beats and ask students to repeat sequence.
   - Stress visual sequence of events or tasks during perceptual and art activities.

- Help the students make lists of the events that took place in a television program. Lead the class in a discussion to reach consensus about the order of the events.
- Tell the class the order of events in the plot of a story.
- Have the group generate individual or group stories, with the teacher stressing sequential order or plot.

EVALUATION METHOD
Product analysis
Casenotes

LEVELS OF APPROPRIATENESS
Best with higher-functioning students or with heterogeneous groups. With lower-functioning students, acting out the sequences may be helpful.

VARIATIONS
Many variations are possible, based on various stimuli suggested by the teacher or students (e.g., describe plot in fairy tales, ghost stories, comic books, cartoons, movies).

COMMENTS
Almost all students we work with who are verbal at all have at least one television show they enjoy and can describe.

Activity D.2: The Adventures of Detective Danny

PRIMARY GOAL
To increase students' awareness of the environments in which they live

SECONDARY GOAL
To increase students' abilities to describe the environment, utilizing the concept of plot

STRATEGY
1. Show the class a large felt board with footprints leading to a house and say, "There is a mystery. Pretend you are Detective Dan, and let's discover whose footprints these are."

2. Continue, "What happened to the person?" As soon as a student responds, say to him or her, "Let's start at the beginning."
3. The teacher wants to be sure that this story illustrates consecutive sequential thought.
4. Stress affective response from the student.
5. Reinforce the concepts of *characters* and *plot*.
6. Have the students write their own group or individual stories, stressing plot aspects.

EVALUATION METHOD
Anecdotes
Product analysis

LEVELS OF APPROPRIATENESS
Best with higher-functioning students or with heterogeneous groups

VARIATIONS
The teacher can make up a variety of "mystery" stories, or get the class to make them up and share them with each other.

Activity D.3: Hypothetical Situations

PRIMARY GOAL
To increase students' awareness of the environments in which they live

SECONDARY GOAL
To increase students' general knowledge about hypothetical situations

STRATEGY
1. Present a hypothetical situation to the class. (For example, "John, you have just won the prize for the best _____.")
2. Ask the student to fill in the missing word.
3. Discuss hypothetical situation. Use two hypothetical situations as a beginning point to tell a story.
4. Encourage specific and varied responses from class members.

EVALUATION METHOD
Product analysis

Casenotes
Anecdotes

LEVELS OF APPROPRIATENESS
All levels

VARIATIONS
Many variations are possible based on the students' abilities in verbal expression, and the stimuli provided by the teacher.

COMMENTS
This basic complete-the-sentence technique can be used in conjunction with many other activities in this book.

Activity D.4: Plot—Comic Books

PRIMARY GOAL
To increase students' abilities to organize their perceptions of the environment

SECONDARY GOAL
To increase students' abilities to describe events in their environments, with emphasis on aspects of sequential order (plot)

STRATEGY
1. Tell the class to draw an "action" picture.
2. When that is done, ask the students to describe what happened.
3. Ask them to add captioned dialogue (help them if necessary).
4. Bring into class comic books and comic strips.
5. Discuss beginning and end of story.
6. Tell the class that the events that happen are *plot*.
7. Emphasize that the point of comic books is there is a minimum of words; the pictures are self-explanatory.
8. Have class members make a short "comic book" or comic strip.

EVALUATION METHOD
Product analysis (of writings and pictures)
Casenotes

Habilitative arts therapy encourages engagement in a variety of art forms, both as a starting point to elicit creative writing and as therapeutic modes in and of themselves.

LEVELS OF APPROPRIATENESS
All levels. With lower-functioning students, emphasis should be on the pictures themselves, with the sequential aspects kept very simple. The teacher may want to use two-step plots, with simple pictures (e.g., a picture of an egg, followed by a picture of a newly hatched chicken). The teacher may want to bring in simple sequential pictures, rather than have the class draw or paint them themselves. (For example, pictures from coloring books could be used, with the group coloring them after they are arranged in order. The teacher could lead a discussion with the class about what is happening in the pictures while the class colors. The action description can be written down and put together to make a group story.)

VARIATIONS
In addition to the variation described above, many others are possible based on the teacher's and students' imaginations and the stimulus

material that is brought to class. If the teacher has taken photographs of a class activity (especially instant-developing pictures), the photos can be substituted for the pictures, and the class can arrange the photos into proper sequence while telling a story about what occurred during the class event.

COMMENTS

This is one of the most flexible activities contained in this book and can be used to follow up almost any class activity or to emphasize content material from other class subjects (e.g., even math could be emphasized in this activity by having the class make up sequential comics or simple books similar to commercially available "counting books"). This activity can also be used to integrate other arts activities, such as music, dance, or sculpture. The students would first participate in the other arts, then make a comic strip of the experience.

Activity D.5: Loud and Soft Beats (Establishment of Rhythmic Patterns in Poetry)

PRIMARY GOAL
To improve students' general expressive abilities

SECONDARY GOAL
To introduce the concept of rhythm in simple poems

STRATEGY
1. Demonstrate clapping hands in simple rhythm emphasizing loud and soft beats.
2. Ask the students to join in.
3. Same as above except using drums and rhythm instruments.
4. Have the students say "loud" or "soft" as they hit the appropriate beat.
5. Introduce a rhythmic song when students are familiar with emphasizing beat.
6. Introduce a poem (spoken) to a simple beat.
7. Ask students to recite a simple rhyme they may know to a simple beat. (It may take various amounts of structuring depending on the class.)

8. Ask each student to make up his or her own simple poem emphasizing loud and soft beats.
9. Reinforce concept by reading simply rhythmic poems to class.

EVALUATION METHOD
Casenotes
Product analysis

LEVELS OF APPROPRIATENESS
All levels. With lower-functioning students, the emphasis should be on the physical involvement with creating or joining in with the rhythm of the examples used in class.

VARIATIONS
Popular songs or other music of the students' choosing can be used to stimulate the rhythmic involvement. This is a good opportunity to let students bring in favorite records or choose music from the class collection.

COMMENTS
Depending on the abilities of students, the teacher may want to stress that not all poems are rhythmic. Explaining that poems are different from stories because they are "packed with more feelings and images" may be helpful. In many cases the best way to get across the point about the difference is simply through reading a variety of free verse poems, as well as a variety of short stories. Some students will be able to tell the difference; others will not. With classes primarily of lower-functioning students it may be best to concentrate on poems that *rhyme* and not get into nonrhyming or nonrhythmical poems.

Activity D.6: Aids to the Teaching of Rhyme

PRIMARY GOAL
To improve students' general expressive abilities

SECONDARY GOAL
To increase students' abilities to use rhymes in poems

STRATEGY

1. Read funny rhyming poems to the class.
2. While discussing the poem, point out which words rhyme.
3. Tell the class, poems sometimes rhyme but not always. All poems do not have to rhyme.
4. Choose a word that is easy to make a rhyme with, and write it on the chalkboard. There will be many factors involved in choosing the word, depending on the level of academic functioning. If the class has no reading skills or is at a very early stage of reading, choose simple word families, such as *an* or *all*. If the class has no reading skills, do the assignment verbally. (For example, "The word we will use is *all*. Who can name a word that rhymes with *all*?")
5. Make a list of the responses (e.g., *all, call, ball, fall, hall, mall, tall,* and *wall*).
6. Say, "Let's all make a poem using these rhyming words. I will make the first line. 'I was playing with my ball.'"
7. Ask the class to help you with the next line, pointing out that they must use one of the words that rhymes with ball. Review the words once more. If the class has problems understanding how to use rhyme, structure your directions so that you make the next line with their help, as follows: Repeat the first line. Tell the class you want to end the next line with the word *call*. Say the words of the first line rhythmically, clapping your hands as you say each syllable. Then clap for each syllable of the second line, saying only "*Call:* ------ call." Feed them the second line if there is still confusion. "And I heard my mother call."
8. Go through this procedure many times until the class begins to understand what is expected. Use the word families as enrichment in their reading program if they are not already familiar with the words. Continue to read many rhyming poems to the class. (Dr. Seuss books are excellent and fun for young children.)

EVALUATION METHOD
Casenotes
Product analysis

LEVELS OF APPROPRIATENESS
All levels

VARIATIONS
Many variations are possible, based on the teacher's input, the students' imaginations, and their progress across time.

COMMENTS
Once the students begin to grasp this concept, they usually enjoy this activity a great deal. It is an activity that should be done with a good deal of emphasis on fun and a fast pace. Group poems can be created fairly quickly with the teacher providing a stimulus word and the students calling out rhyming words in brainstorm fashion as the teacher writes. These poems may resemble nonsense verses and enable input from all students, even those who may not contribute rhyming words. As an example, the following excerpt is from a poem created by a heterogeneous group of students from severely retarded to low-average intelligence:

> Chuck the Duck — Luckity Luck.
> Chuck the Duck, Fell in the Muck . . .
> Chuck the Duck, Had No Luck.
> Bang! Bang!

Activity D.7: Music—Song Writing

PRIMARY GOAL
To increase students' general expressive abilities

SECONDARY GOAL
To improve students' abilities to express themselves, through the creation of simple songs

STRATEGY
1. Hand out rhythm instruments.
2. Ask the students to bang or clap a simple beat.
3. Tell the class, "We will make up a song." Ask the students what they would like to sing about. If they don't know, begin making up a song about them, encouraging them to continue. Try to keep it centered on the students themselves.
4. Always use a tape recorder for this activity.

5. Play back the tape for the class.
6. Write down their lyrics and read them to the class.
7. Work with each student on the lyrics if they are not satisfied with them.
8. Students should keep a collection of their music in their anthologies.

EVALUATION METHOD
Casenotes
Product analysis

LEVELS OF APPROPRIATENESS
All levels

VARIATIONS
Have the students make up new lyrics to an already existing melody

COMMENTS
This is another activity that should be kept lively and fast-paced, with brainstorming by students that the teacher then helps organize into a song format. With higher-functioning groups, or as the students become more experienced, the teacher will need to provide less guidance and/or structure.

Activity D.8: Writing Haiku

PRIMARY GOAL
To increase students' general expressive ability

SECONDARY GOAL
To increase students' ability to use imagery in writing

STRATEGY
1. Explain to the class that a *haiku* is a traditional form of Japanese poetry. It consists of three lines and seventeen syllables and is derived from the Buddist tradition. A haiku utilizes imagery in such a way that there is immediate understanding (i.e., instant enlightenment in Buddist tradition).

2. Read traditional haiku to class. Discuss the imagery.
3. Refer to painting with words — this is an example of a simple and literal use.
4. Read more haiku.
5. Have the class try to write haiku.

EVALUATION METHOD
Casenotes
Product analysis (Note that the emphasis is *not* necessarily the product of the haiku, per se, but the use of imagery.)

LEVELS OF APPROPRIATENESS
This is best with higher-functioning groups of students.

VARIATIONS
The teacher may assist the class in getting started by creating short haiku, leaving off the last word or two, and asking the students to complete them. Once they begin to feel confident and get the basic idea, the teacher can write shorter and shorter portions of each haiku, while assisting the students in keeping track of the number of syllables, if necessary. Eventually the students may be able to create their own haiku without assistance.

COMMENTS
Although haiku are difficult to write exactly according to traditional form, they are excellent for encouraging the use of imagery. The teacher should not make a major attempt to keep the syllables exactly to seventeen or the lines to exactly three. The two haiku that follow are good examples of technically imperfect haiku that were created without any teacher assistance by two mildly retarded students:

> The bird flew down and put his feet on the muddy water
> Then he flew to his nest
> And the little boy came and saw it.

> The sunset goes down
> The sky is real clear
> And very quiet.

Activity D.9: Novels and Short Stories

PRIMARY GOAL
To increase students' abilities to organize their expressive efforts

SECONDARY GOAL
To familiarize students with the basic difference between novels and short stories

STRATEGY
1. Discuss with students the difference between novels and short stories. Here are some ideas:
   - Short stories usually take place in one time period. They are not long so the author must choose things about the character that will stand out in a reader's mind. For example, children's stories are often really short stories, and we don't know everything about the characters except what is important to the story. For instance, all we really know about Hansel and Gretel is that their stepmother is mean and they want to go home.
   - In a novel, which takes place over a longer time span, we know much more about the characters. For example, we know a great deal about Dorothy from the Wizard of Oz because the author had time to develop her life and background.
   - Novels are analogous to movies (two hours or more), and short stories are analogous to thirty-minute weekly television shows.
2. Have students write short stories, giving emphasis to the most important things about the characters to relate to the reader.
3. Students should not be expected to write novels but novel reading should become part of classwork as well as short stories, with discussion of the characters in each, as well as the plot and theme.

EVALUATION METHOD
Product analysis
Casenotes

LEVELS OF APPROPRIATENESS
Appropriate only with highest-functioning students

VARIATIONS

With students who can read independently, the teacher may ask that they report to the class about the stories or novels they have read. A simple checklist could be made to use in discussing character, plot, and theme with the class (e.g., Who are the characters? What are the major events that occurred — plot? What is the lesson or moral of the story or novel — theme?). The teacher can read stories or novels to the students (whether or not they can read), pointing out the same elements: character, plot, theme.

COMMENTS

As in the other activities, it is not acquiring the specific information that is critical, but the process of getting students interested in various forms of expression that they may not previously have been exposed to. It may be helpful to generate a small class library of appropriate and interesting books that the students would like to read or that the teacher could read to the entire class.

CHAPTER 5

Selected Creative Writings of Students

Writings included in this chapter represent a broad spectrum of styles and content. They were written over a period of ten years by clients who were functionally mentally retarded or severely disabled cognitively, because of emotional disturbance, learning disability, brain damage, or cultural deprivation. These people were receiving services in a variety of programs at either a state institution for the mentally retarded or a community-based educational center for emotionally disturbed children.

In all cases the clients were not able to function in public school classes, usually because of their behavioral or emotional problems rather than their intellectual ability. That many of the pieces were written by institutionalized clients will be obvious from their content. Similarly the emotional, social, or behavioral difficulties, as well as the frequently tragic histories, of many of the writers will also become clear.

We are excited by the writings these people produced and believe developmentally delayed students in public schools, whether in special education classes or mainstreamed into the system, could learn to produce writings of equal or better quality. However, we stress that the quality and the content were merely byproducts of the habilitative arts therapy process.

A word is necessary about the selection process. We had considered including a sample of one or more writings that were generated by each of the techniques described in the manual. However, we felt the sequence and the beauty of many of the works would be lost if arranged in that manner. Additionally there is a diversity of style, content, theme, and quality of works generated by any one technique, especially when used in a group of writers. We realized that there was no logic to "matching up" a writing to each technique because the techniques are primarily jumping-off points to stimulate interest and enthusiasm and to help the writer to structure his or her own thoughts. The works that result are often not predictable and represent the individuality of each writer. In fact, it is the ability of the techniques to catalyze individuality that gives them their value in the creative process.

The writings that follow have been chosen because they are indicative of various styles by the developmentally delayed people. Often the grammar is incorrect, the thoughts may be vague, yet the emotional quality comes through. Although they were originally written through a variety of techniques, they have been organized by theme to show the divergence of production.

PERSONAL STATEMENTS

The first group of writings is characterized by the authors' strong personal statements. Writing on this personal level can only be achieved when the environment assures trust and safety.

The author of the following poem is a developmentally delayed male, age twenty-seven, who is institutionalized.

ME

I'm good at reading,
Finding girls,
And eating.
I'm real good at work,
Folding papers and listening.
I listen very well.
I draw better than anyone else.
I draw houses, buildings, and people.
I draw people on paper a whole lot.
I draw Jeff, Libby, and God.
Paint brushes make me sad —

I can't paint.
My fingers don't move right.
I can't handle my brain tumor and I can't write good.
I guess I'm a good person,
Loving and kind,
I'm a loyal friend.

The following two poems were created by an eighteen-year-old woman, developmentally delayed, who after many years of institutionalization now resides in a community-based group home.

IF I COULD BE . . .

If I could be,
I'd be Donna Fargo.
I'd be . . .
THE HAPPIEST GIRL IN THE WHOLE USA.

GRANDMOTHER

A couple of weeks ago my Grandmother passed away
    about one thirty when she was taking her medicine.
They called my Momma.
Sad.
I was more closer than anybody.
Makes me feel like crying.
Like I was her child.
I really love my grandmother!
I couldn't talk about it.
The more I talked the more it hurt.
When I was two or three years old,
She took me.
I loved her like she was my Momma.
She always had a big jar of candy for me.
Round and brown.
She always gave me whippings,
Cause she loved me.
When I think about it, I want to
Cry.

The two pieces that follow were created by an eighteen-year-old, developmentally delayed man with cerebral palsy. He is semiambulatory.

THE WAY THE WORLD IS

Before I came to the Center when I was at home, my foster family used to woop me for something I could not help. They knew that I could not walk but they would woop me anyway. I really didn't understand it because I was young.

Portrait of Ted, painted by a twenty-seven-year-old mentally retarded male.

I was five and a half (a year before I came here). We were going to church, walking to the car with my foster mother. Walking out of the house I fell and she slapped me. I couldn't understand why. I have Cerebral Palsy which makes my muscles not work. She didn't know I had Cerebral Palsy, but she knew I couldn't walk.

I came to the Center in February 1969. For two or three years, I didn't go home. After that I had home visits with my foster parents. And then when I went home they started being mean to me again. They would fuss at me and tell me to walk. They made me walk with my walker. They would make me walk in the hot sun. It shocked me when they treated me like that. Shocked and sad.

They claimed they loved me, but they did very bad things to me. It made me cry. I didn't like them at the time. It got so bad that I had to call my real mother and have her bring me back to the Center. I couldn't be with my real mother because she has back trouble and she couldn't take care of me. So she gave me up when I was four. The real reason she had to give me up was because after I was born, my real daddy left and she was alone.

Even though I didn't love them then, I love 'em now. Because they don't woop me no more and don't fuss at me. I see them about once a month.

It's weird — because sometimes I was beaten so much when I was young. Sometimes I'm scared when I first meet somebody, but after I get to know them and know that they won't hurt me, I begin to love and get closer to them. But don't get me wrong, nobody loves everybody and I sure don't. Some people are good and some are bad. That's just the way it is in this world.

WHAT GETTING OFF MEANS

Some people think that beating your meat or having sex is the only way of getting off. But anything that takes you away from anger or being mad or being sad, anything that makes you feel good, doesn't hurt yourself or anyone else, and gives you a good feeling inside, that is another way of getting off.

A twenty-six-year-old, mentally retarded person who has been institutionalized for seventeen years composed the poem below.

LOVE

People love children and everybody!
Everybody should love people.
Be nice and kind,
And don't ever try fights or do something wrong.
Cause you might be in jail,
or worse than that the devil.
You should love people.
Nice and kind.
Then you might go to heaven,
And meet Jesus.
When you go to heaven,
You might love animals, people and angels.
The whole works.
Don't go the devil.
Try to make it to God.

The author of the following two pieces is an institutionalized man in his thirties with moderate mental retardation and accompanying emotional problems.

HARD FACTS OF COTTAGE LIFE

Well, I only been in only one place,
It's been here.
I hit a boy one time,
And he's got $4.00 worth of brain damage,
$4.00 worth of brain damage!
Not much goes on . . .
I get up every morning,
Brush my teeth,
Comb my hair—everything!
These are the facts of life!

MY DADDY

One time, I was crying for my daddy.
He's dead a long time.
Dead and gone.
He's dead. He don't know I'm here.
And guess what?
When he comes back on judgement day, he'll find out.
He'll find out he'll want to take me home.
But when he takes me home he'll find out
I prayed for the good Lord to take him to Heaven.

The following two pieces were the work of a seventeen-year-old woman who is mildly retarded with severe emotional problems.

A FAMILY

I really do wish I had me a family,
In Florida.
A nice warm house.
Me and my husband,
And a little boy and a little girl.
Maybe twins.
Get me a job.
To pay for the children, and the house.
A brick house.
To keep nice and warm.
My own swimming pool.

THE KINDA MOMMA I WANNA BE

I'd like to be the kinda momma who likes to keep all the children who can't have a momma and daddy . . . who don't have a nice family or one who cares about them. I don't really know what kinda momma you'd call this.

I'd like to be the kinda momma who cares about children . . . like all the boys who have daddies who don't care about them.

I find them . . . love them . . . keep them warm. . . .
I don't know what the name would be. Those kind of parents
who don't care a bit about their children and don't wanna
keep them and they put them in a home.
Yes . . . some day I wanna be a momma . . . someday. . . .

A sixteen-year-old male with multiple disabilities that render him
nonambulatory created the two poems below.

THINKING ABOUT A FRIEND

I walk thru rains,
And it makes me feel sad,
Cause the boy has problems.
People can get sad,
When they have a death.
When sad music comes on,
At the funeral home,
It makes you want to cry.
You won't see that person again.
When you sleep and don't
      ever wake up again.

MOMMA

When I was a baby my mother left me.
Somebody left me in the crib.
When I wanted out, I started crying.

Something came in the window and made me really scared.
I still don't know what it was.

My mother took care of me for a while before I
      was admitted to Western Carolina Center.
I don't want her ever to come back and see me.
She wasn't a very good mother.
At that time the only thing I could say was,
Momma
      Momma
            Momma.

Duck, sculpted from papier-maché by a group of severely to moderately retarded adolescents.

The author of the next three poems is a seventeen-year-old, functionally retarded man. He suffers from muscular dystrophy that allows him only to move his head and two fingers.

MY CASE HISTORY

I got left in the house when I was a baby,
By myself (about age six).
When I went out of the house I didn't see anybody.
A policeman picked me up and took me to the Asheville police
    department.
I felt scared, strange and frustrated. They called a lot
    of places for me to stay. A woman took me.
It was so long ago I don't remember who it was.

> I wonder why my mother left me?
> I shouldn't have been treated like that.
> I was just a little kid.

I didn't know what to do.
Makes you want to sit down and cry!

I was crying so much
I couldn't keep from getting nervous.
I was crawling on my hands and knees.
I couldn't walk.
Scared to death!

WHEN I GET MAD I GET GLAD

When I get mad, I always cuss myself out
And sometimes I cuss the staff out.
After I get finished hollering,
I feel a hundred percent better.
When my angries is gone, I feel a hundred percent better.
That's it.

EASTER

Easter is a beautiful day,
It makes you think about Jesus.
How fascinating the way
He healed people.
If I saw him,
I'd ask him to heal me.

The following two pieces are the work of a fourteen-year-old, functionally retarded, severely antisocial female.

MY DADDY

He was a very nice person. When he was at home, before he died, he told us when he died that he hopes that when we grow up we'd be like him. He's got five kids. He's got five sisters and three brothers. He had three dogs, and on weekends we'd go spend the weekend with him. Now we wish we could see him again; and show him how much we've grown up. We still remember the things that he used to do for us. It was very

sad to see him die. What makes me mad is no one ever told
me when he died, I had to wait until I got home until I found
out! I still dream at night that I see him.

THE CEMETERY

There's people buried in the cemetery. And their family visits them. How much they wish they could see them again. Just
like I wish I could see my grandmother again. That means
their feelings are still inside of you, you can remember the
things they did and you never forget the things they did before
they died.

I went to my grandmother's funeral. It is very sad to go to
funerals; you cry alot.

At night when I go to sleep, I dream about my grandfather.
Things that he did for all of his grandkids were very nice.
He'd take us to the store. He'd take us for walks. Then at
night when we'd go to bed, he'd tell us stories of back in the
old days. My grandfather was in the Army, it says on his tomb
that he was in the Army. When it rained we stayed in the
house and watched T.V. together. I remember a lot of things
about my grandfather.

The last writing in this section is by a twenty-six-year-old woman
who suffers from cerebral palsy. The only means of communication
for her is the use of the symbol board; she must indicate the desired
word by the movement of her head as someone points to each symbol.

MY LIFE

"This book is dedicated to all the people that I love."

I was born April 22, 1954. I was born at Rutherford Hospital. I was in the hospital many days. My stay in the hospital
lasted fourteen days.

I went back to the hospital in Rutherfordton when I was 3
years old. They did not think I would be alive at three years
old. The reason they thought this was because my mother had
a lot of pain when I was born. I was deprived of oxygen at

birth and I stayed in an incubator for a week. After fourteen days I went home. I lived at home for eight years. Those eight years were many good years of my life.

I loved the house that I lived in. There were nine people who lived in that house. They were Mama, Daddy, Dorothy, Marion, Mary, Brenda, Martha, Doug, and me. I was the baby. We did many happy things together. We watched T.V. We went to the movies together. We were a happy family. I loved my family.

One time Dorothy, Mother and I went to Virginia. That was when my father was working in Virginia. My brother had a house there. He wanted my father to help work on the house.

We went to Virginia in the winter time. At my brother's house, we got snowed in for three days. We were not able to go out anywhere! We were not even able to visit my sister who also lives in Virginia. We told her we were sorry but she was disappointed anyway. After the snow melted, we went home.

We had a difficult winter that year. That winter I had a lot of problems with my throat. I had a lot of pain. That year we went to Virginia nine times. We went to Virginia a lot because my sister was in the hospital.

I loved my sister Mary's house. It was a small house. It had three rooms in it. My brother had a bigger house with five rooms in it. Marion also had a house with five rooms in it. Dorothy lived at my house. Dorothy and I had a room together. We were good pals.

I came to Western Carolina Center when I was eight years old. I have been at the Center for thirteen years.

I was in A Area when I first came to Western Carolina Center. Ronnie F. was working in A Area then. We went to see a concert in Charlotte. Ronnie did a lot of things with the group that I lived with. He took us to the movies, on bus rides, on picnics, to dances, and to summer camp. I think Ronnie is a good worker here at Western Carolina Center. I think he is funny. Ronnie is my good friend.

Three years ago I moved to H Area. I had a hard time moving to H Area. I had many good friends in A Area. I think I am lucky to be in H Area now. I feel that I am an important person in H Area. Being treated like a child is something I don't like. That is what I did not like about being in A Area.

In January of 1979, I got some bad news about my mother. I was at school in the morning. I got a call to go to Marieta H.'s office. She was my social worker at the time. When I got to Marieta's office, my sister Dorothy was there with her husband. Martha, another sister, was also there. They told me that Mama died. I was extremely upset. I cried but I had a hard time believing what they said. I just could not believe that my Mama was dead. I went to her funeral on January 10.

Often I get a sad feeling inside of me thinking about Mama being dead, but I still have the rest of my family and I care for them.

My sister Dorothy often comes to get me and takes me home with her. She came this past Thanksgiving and took me home. I really enjoy going home to see my family. I remember when I was a little girl and lived at home. I wish I could go home more often, but I realize going home is hard on them. I am a big girl now and taking care of me is really hard on Dorothy. Even though I don't get to go home as much as I used to, I still love my family and I know they love me.

End.

EXPRESSIONS OF ART EXPERIENCES

The arts as an experience are often directly reflected in creative writing. The following pieces were stimulated directly by one or more of the arts experiences.

The author of the first two works is a seventeen-year-old, functionally retarded male. He suffers from muscular dystrophy, which allows him only to move his head and two fingers.

A VERY EXCELLENT PAINTING: GUERNICA BY PICASSO

It's very frightening. Shooting, bombing and all that jazz.

Everybody was screaming and falling to the ground; screaming their guts out cause bombs were falling, tearing the town up. They were horrified and couldn't strike back at them. Airplanes bombing; the first time it ever happened.

Disgusted, real frightened,
Hearts beat real fast,
People trying to get out in a hurry.
When they tried to run,
They fell down dead,
Every second.

Picasso was trying to explain for the whole wide world that war is disgusting. Blood and guts make you feel awful. Mostly wars happen but he says it isn't right. I agree 100% on that. He's right!

IN A DARK ALLEY: A BEETHOVEN SONATA

In a dark alley
Moving slow in slow motion.
Feels like you can't see anything.
It's frightening.
By yourself.
Afraid of the dark
in the dark night,
people get killed.
Dark grey skies floating in air.
Slow concentrated motion
    moving down slowly.
Aiming toward the ground.

The poem below was composed by an eighteen-year-old, brain-damaged person who suffers from multiple handicaps and is rendered semiambulatory.

ATONAL MUSIC—HALLOWEEN

Dark shadows
Slowly
Coming toward me.
Chop my head off.
Halloween night.
Twelve midnight

Ghost
Witches
Bats
flying around my head.
Creepy
Weird
Strange
Scared
They got teeth
Suck your blood.

The following, jointly written, lyric poems were authored by two developmentally delayed individuals aged twenty-six and twenty-seven.

A SILLY SONG ABOUT A FISH

There are 100 fish swimming in the lake.
Bald-headed fish, termite fish, fish that are
    friends with frogs.
There are talking fish.
We think it's crazy to talk to fish.

One fish went in, one fish went out.
Tell a joke about fish.
Let's catch fish with a great big hook.
Yum, yum, yum.

IMAGERY: MOONLIGHT SONATA

People dying in a ghetto.
Cause they have no education.
When they were little they never
had a good mama and daddy.
Someone who loves you.
Don't beat you.
Try their best to teach you right from wrong.
Dirty.
The man who lives in the ghetto is poor.

Still Life in Prison, painted by a twenty-seven-year-old mentally retarded male.

The author of the next two poems is a twenty-seven-year-old, mentally retarded male.

IMAGERY: MOONLIGHT SONATA II

A man playing a piano.
Tall with a red coat.
He feels real bad.
Cause he can't handle money.
He has a tumor.
He's going to die for others.
It scares him.
Because he belongs to God.
He wants to live.
So he keeps always up.
It's both true and a lie.

THE DANCE FESTIVAL (THE ALVIN AILEY DANCERS)

They danced up and down.
Round and round
Even moving seats
Slow and fast and medium music.
Black and white dancers.
Dressed in white and blue
Moving fast
Angling umbrellas
Pushing
Spinning
Making me feel real good!

An eighteen-year-old, brain-damaged person who suffers from multiple handicaps and is partially ambulatory expressed the poem below.

CREATION OF THE WORLD BY MILHAUD

When there was nothing so black
You couldn't see
God decided: "I wonder what it
would be like to have light?"
So He said: "Let there be light."
Creeping like a turtle
Slowly but surely
It got light.
Orange and red and beautiful.
In the morning like a yellow-
    orange ball,
The sun rises to give us light.

The author of the following poem is a thirty-two-year-old, mentally retarded male, who now resides in a community group home.

THE NEW ELVIS

Might be sent to Washington, D.C.
Gonna be a movie star!

Gonna sing Hound Dog!
Elvis makes new record!
Elvis looks fine!
I'M TAKING OVER!
Somebody'll put me on a T.V. set.
But I don't know what channel.
August the fourth, 1976.
LOVE ME TENDER
LOVE ME TRUE
LOVE ME LIKE A FOOL.

The poem below was a group creation by four mentally retarded persons ranging in age from fourteen years to twenty-six years.

IMAGERY — AFTER LISTENING
TO ORFEO AND ERUDICE BY GLUCK

I feel lonely when I have nothing to do
I get frustrated when I have nothing to do
I feel like I float in air
When I'm lonely I feel like flying
But I can't.

I would feel sad if the grey skies were falling.
Sometimes when the full moon comes out it is
A bright night.
Sometimes it's a black night
I feel lonely when darkness and blackness comes.
In my mind I feel ocean waters moving in.

Black sea and black night
Feel like a bad night
Sad because people's hearts are breaking
I feel crowded, sad, and homesick
Sometimes like a black night.

Wanted to cry
Rain falling
Very cloudy outside

Cold and windy
The ocean moving round like sea that's scary
Like sea that's scary
Like waves moving up and down
Back and forth.

People
Slowly
Dancing ballet.

Lonely like waving clouds
Like a storm
Grey clouds
Feel like it's dark.

Trees are blowing
Wind is blowing
Sky is black
Trees and sky waving
Black night.

The following piece is by an eighteen-year-old, brain-damaged person who suffers from multiple handicaps and is rendered nonambulatory.

JONATHAN LIVINGSTON SEAGULL

Jonathan Livingston Seagull wanted to fly. He wanted to go as fast as his wings could take him. He fell because he was way up in the sky and the wind knocked him down. He hit the water and started all over again. He went back to his flock to tell his friends that he would never want to stop flying.

His friends said, "Oh, have mercy!"

His mind went black for a minute cause he though they would like it, but they didn't!

John felt sad because nobody agreed with him. He hates that no one likes him. He hates that no one agreed with him. He was afraid no one would feed him. He has to fly because he can't stop!

POEMS ABOUT DREAMS

Dreams can be a rich source of creativity for handicapped students. The following poems were written after a discussion about dreams.

The authors of the first two poems are eighteen-year-old, brain-damaged persons who suffer from multiple handicaps and are rendered semiambulatory.

A DREAM

I dreamed one night that I was floating.
It felt funny like you might fall.
It was scary to have no one underneath to catch you.
It also felt like someone was calling my name.
I believe it was a cottage parent.
"Jerry, Jerry, Jerry."
Finally, I awoke.
I told them the dream.
They stayed with me for a while.
I was really scared.

A DREAM

I thought about a woman.
She was real pretty, with black hair,
    and dark skin and thin.
I met this woman and we got married.
We stayed married two years.
We had two twins and we started having problems.
So we went our separate ways.
More than likely that would happen to me.

A seventeen-year-old, brain-damaged man who has been institutionalized for many years composed the poem below.

I DREAMED ABOUT GROWING UP

I was growing up
I dreamed about money and a suitcase.

I dreamed about a pair of shoes.
I dreamed about some money.
I dreamed about watches and stuff.
I dreamed about clothes with money in them.
Trying to get me a job.
Trying to get me a big bag of apples.
Eating fish
Eating moonpies.

FANTASY PIECES

The last group of writings deals thematically with active imagination, wishes, and hopes: the stuff of which literature is made.

The poem below was created by a seventeen-year-old, functionally retarded man who suffers from muscular dystrophy.

IMAGINATION

Imagination is a wonderful thing.
If I could eat again I'd eat everything in the store.
I'd eat soup, beans, pinto beans, slaw and corn bread.
That would make real fine meal for me.
Some nights I imagine I eat.
Some nights I imagine I eat milkshakes, hamburgers and
    french fries.
Now I eat from a tube attached to the wall of my stomach.
Imagination makes me feel like I could walk but I can't
    do it.

The author of the following two pieces is a seventeen-year-old, mildly retarded woman with severe emotional problems.

A BIRD

Living near my house.
I'd like to have a nice yellow bird.
So I could hear him whistling.

The Owl, painted by a seventeen-year-old mildly retarded woman with emotional problems.

Singing songs.
Love songs, in the sunlight.
Me and my husband on the porch swinging.
It's spring time.
Thinking bout a picnic
Hearing the bird sing.

THE BIRD

The bird's Mommy and Daddy were fussing and fighting and all—and when the bird always did something bad, the mother came out and whipped her and didn't feed it. The baby bird cried, cried, and cried. One day when the father came, the bird was real thin and was so hungry that the father bird got real angry at the mother bird and took the baby bird away to the bird's grandmother. He told the grandmother bird to call him if the mother bird tried to come take the baby bird away.

The baby bird was nervous and scared that the mother bird might find her at the grandmother's. Then the baby bird lived there 'til he learned to fly away and find a happy place. He wanted to find a happy place instead of having the mother around telling him what to do.

The bird wished he could hurry up and grow up like a big boy and live where he wanted to and have children of his own.

Then the baby bird told his grandmother and father his wish of what would happen to him and one day the wish came true and he said goodbye to his grandmother and father and flew away, way, way far away.

Then the baby bird hoped his mother could change a lot and turn out to be a good mother bird.

The composition below is by an eighteen-year-old, brain-damaged person who suffers from multiple handicaps.

I LIKE TO GET OFF TO HARD ROCK

Made me feel good. It made me get excited with all the men and women screaming. Everytime they yell, "play, play some more," I get happier and happier, and I keep beating the hell out of the bongos. The sweat was rolling off me like I'd been in the shower. I had on a black shirt, it was real silky and I had on a pair of black blue jeans. They weren't silk, but they were real nice. I had on a fancy blue jean jacket, and two rings, and a cross, and my braces. I had so much money, I could get it (braces) special made and had high heeled boots and had the braces hooked into the heels somehow. And I was on tour and been on tour for a year. And the fans loved me and it was a sell out. But it made me feel good, because after playing for two hours, after I went back to the dressing room, the fans went crazy. Started beating on the chairs and kept yelling, "more, more bongo kid, more, more." And I didn't want to come out because I wanted to go back home to Las Vegas where my mansion is. Because I was tired and rock stars don't eat good while on the road, and I was doing three shows in one day for a whole year. I was making big cash, getting off, getting that good feeling.

It made me feel good cause all of my performances hadn't been like this. They hadn't all been successful. But two things that helped me be successful, that I could play the bongos, but something else that made me more famous was playing the congo drums without a stick, with my fingers. I was the first one to do that. And when people saw that they went crazier than hell cause I had done something no one else had done. I pick up the congo drums and I picked it up plumb over my head. I was holding it and hopping with it at the same time. I slammed it on the stage and once more beat the hell out of it. The fans called me out, but I was tired and didn't want to come out for the fourth time. But when you're out in California, Los Angeles, California and its a sell out and you got 500,000 the biggest auditorium out there, and the very biggest and if you're a real entertainer, you can't turn that down. The last thing I want to say, is I loved it so much that it put me in the hospital. I was married in this dream, but I loved music so much that it broke it up in less than a year. But if you're wondering why I mention all of the hard things, like being on the road, and not eating, is cause a rock star's life ain't easy. But I love it so much, the last thing I want to say, I let it break up my marriage and you might think this is crazy, but I loved it so much that it was worth going to the hospital and having a broken marriage and having poor health. If you're a true musician, you'll be willing to suffer all the bad things for your music. And that's what a true musician is. If you don't love it that much, and I'm not trying to sound like I know it all, but if you're a true musician you'll be willing to suffer all the bad things, for if you're a true musician. The end.

Post script —

But it didn't really happen, it was just a dream . . . but it might someday; it really might!!!!

APPENDIX
BIBLIOGRAPHY
INDEX

Sample Data Sheets

The data sheets in this section are provided to serve as examples of useful methods of data collection. The reader is encouraged to adapt each one to the individual characteristics of the classroom and to the individual needs of his or her students.

FIGURE 1. A FORMAT FOR EVENT RECORDING

BEHAVIOR BASELINE

Student _____ Location_____

Instructions: Record the date, time, and frequency of each target behavior emitted by the
   student.

Behavior(s) to be observed:

_____

_____

_____

_____

_____

Behavior	Date	Time: From—till	Frequency	Comments	Observer's Initials

Note: This data sheet may be used for simple event recording during initial phases. (Baseline data is taken during first sessions before treatment has presumably changed the behavior. Later results are then compared with the baseline data.)

148

FIGURE 2

RANDOM TIME SAMPLING

Client _____

Setting_____ Date_____ Time_____

Key: Target Behaviors (List behaviors chosen for measurement.)

A =

B =

C =

D =

E =

Instructions: In the boxes below, which represent five-second intervals, record the letters of the target behaviors that occur within that interval. More than one letter can be recorded in each box, but no letter should be marked more than once per box. Skip five seconds between each recording interval to give yourself time to write.

#1 5 5 5 5 5 5   # 2 5 5 5 5 5 5

#3 5 5 5 5 5 5   # 4 5 5 5 5 5 5

#5 5 5 5 5 5 5   # 6 5 5 5 5 5 5

#7 5 5 5 5 5 5   # 8 5 5 5 5 5. 5

#9 5 5 5 5 5 5   #10 5 5 5 5 5 5

Comments

_____

Signature of Observer

FIGURE 3

STUDENT BEHAVIOR CHECKLIST

Student_____ Teacher_____

Instructions: Assign a rating based on the student's behavior each day.

Target Behavior	Usually Good	Sometimes Good, Sometimes a Problem	Often a Serious Problem
I. *Student's Social Interaction with Others* A. Relations with other students			
B. Relations with family (if known)			
C. Relations with teacher D. Participation in planned activity			
E. Participation with other staff F. General social maturity (e.g., concern for others)			
II. *Student's Task Performance* A. Willingness to participate B. Appropriateness of efforts to contribute			
C. Expressive level attained D. Level of inactivity ("doing nothing") E. Initiative in seeking help from teacher			
F. Ability to criticize own work			

Target Behavior	Usually Good	Sometimes Good, Sometimes a Problem	Often a Serious Problem
III. *Student's Communication*			
A. Initiation of communication			
B. Response to initiation of communication by others			
C. Warmth and feeling in conversation			
D. Willingness to talk about a specific subject as opposed to rambling speech			
E. Willingness to listen to others			
F. Having a helping attitude toward others			
G. Level of self-esteem			
IV. *Student's Physical Health*			
A. General health			
B. Tendency to complain of nonexistent illnesses			
C. Other. Describe:			
V. *Atmosphere in Class as a Whole*			
A. General harmony			
B. Communication among students			
C. Willingness of students to do assigned tasks			

Note: Adapted from Willenson and Bisgaard (1970), "Resident Problems Checklist." Used by permission.

FIGURE 4. A Basic Format for Anecdotal Data

BEHAVIOR INTERACTION RECORD

Client _____ Location _____ Date _____

Time	Behavior Emitted	Surrounding Events	Response/Intervention	Client Response	Observer's Initials

Bibliography

Aiken, L. R. *Psychological testing and assessment* (3rd ed.). Boston: Allyn and Bacon, 1976.

Anderson, E. M. The disabled child at school: Special needs and special provisions. *Birth Defects,* 1976, *12* (4), 47–62.

Arieti, S. The rise of creativity: From primary to tertiary process. *Contemporary Psychoanalysis,* 1964, *1,* 51–68.

————. *Creativity: The magic synthesis.* New York: Basic Books, 1976.

Ayers, B. E., & Duguay, A. R. Critical variables in counseling the mentally retarded. *Rehabilitation Literature,* 1969, *30* (3), 42–44.

Bachelder, B. Needs gratification and contingency management: Compatible or incompatible approaches at Western Carolina Center. Unpublished manuscript, 1979.

Bacher, J. H. The effects of special class placement on self-concept, social adjustment, and reading growth of slow learners (Doctoral dissertation, New York University, 1964). *Dissertation Abstracts,* 1965, 25–7071.

Balla, D., & Zigler, E. Personality development in retarded persons. In N. Ellis (Ed.), *Handbook of mental deficiency, psychological theory and research* (2nd ed.). Hillsdale, N. J.: Lawrence Erlbaum Assoc., 1979, pp. 143–168.

Bank-Mikkelsen, N. E. A metropolitan area in Denmark, Copenhagen. In R. B. Kigel & W. Wolfensberger (Eds.), *U.S. President's Committee on Mental Retardation: Changing patterns in residential services for the mentally retarded.* Washington, D.C.: U.S. Government Printing Office, 1969.

Bauer, R., & Modaressi, T. Strategies of therapeutic contact: Working with children with severe object relationship disturbance. *American Journal of Psychotherapy,* 1977, *31* (4).

Becker, H. Problems of inference and proof in participant observation. *American Sociological Review,* 1958, *23,* 652–660.

Becker, H. S., & Greer, B. Participants observation and interviewing: A comparison. In W. J. Filstead (Ed.), *Qualitative methodology: Firsthand involvement with the social world.* Chicago: Markam, 1970.

Begab, M. J., & Richardson, S. A. (Eds.) *The mentally retarded and society.* Baltimore: University Park Press, 1975.

Bem, D. J. Self-perception: An alternative interpretation of cognitive dissonance phenomena. *Psychological Review*, 1967, *74* (3), 183–200.

Bice, H. V. Some factors that contribute to the concept of self in the child with cerebral palsy. *Mental Hygiene*, 1954, *38*, 120–131.

Billow, R. M. Metaphor: A review of psychological literature. *Psychological Bulletin*, 1978, *1*, 81–92.

Biondi, A. M. (Ed.) *The creative process.* Buffalo, N.Y.: D.O.K., 1972.

Blatt, B. Issues and values. In B. Blatt, D. Biklen, & R. Bogdan (Eds.), *An alternative textbook in special education: People, schools and other institutions.* Denver: Love, 1977.

Blumberg, M. Creative dramatics: An outlet for mental handicaps. *Journal of Rehabilitation*, 1976, *42* (6), 17–20; 40; 48.

Bogdan, R. B., & Taylor, S. A. *Introduction of qualitative research methods.* New York: John Wiley, 1975.

_____. The judged, not the judges: An insider's view of mental retardation. *American Psychologist*, 1976, *31* (1).

Bowlby, J. *Attachment* (Vol. 1). Attachment and Loss. London: Hogarth; New York: Basic Books, 1969.

Branden, N. *The Psychology of Self-Esteem.* Los Angeles: Nash, 1969.

_____. *The Disowned Self.* Los Angeles: Nash, 1972.

Broadbeck, M. *Reading in the philosophy of the social sciences.* New York: Macmillan, 1968.

Brooks, P. H., & Baumeister, A. A. A plea for consideration of ecological validity in the experimental psychology of mental retardation: A guest editorial. *American Journal of Mental Deficiency*, 1977, *81* (5), 407–416.

Bruner, J. *On knowing: Essays for the left hand.* New York: Atheneum, 1968.

Buck, L. A., & Kramer, A. Poetic creativity in deaf children. *American Annals of the Deaf* 1976, *121* (1), 31–37.

_____. Creative potential in schizophrenia. *Psychiatry*, 1977, *40* (May), 146–162.

Burkhart, C. C., & McNeil, H. M. *Identity and teacher learning.* Scranton, Pa.: International Textbook, 1968.

Burrows, A. T., Ferbie, J. D., Jackson, D. C., & Sanders, D. O. *They all want to write.* Englewood Cliffs, N.J.: Prentice-Hall, 1952.

Cady, J. L. Pretend you are an author. *Teaching Exceptional Children.* Fall 1975, pp. 26–31.

Calhoun, G., Jr., & Elliott, R. N., Jr. Self-concept and academic achievement of educable retarded and emotionally disturbed pupils. *Exceptional Children*, 1977, *43* (6), 379–380.

Campbell, D. T. Factors relevant to the validity of experiments in social settings. *Psychological Bulletin*, 1957, *54* (4), 297–313.

Cantwell, D. P. Psychiatric disorder in children with speech and language retardation. *Archives of General Psychiatry*, 1977, *34*, 583–591.

Carr, C. C., & McLaughlin, J. A. Self-concepts of mentally retarded adults in an adult education class. *Mental Retardation*, 1973, *11* (6), 57–59.

Carvajal, A. L. Predictors of four criteria on self concept in educable mentally retarded adolescents. *Exceptional Children*, 1977, *43*, 239.

Craighead, W., Kazdin, A., & Mahoney, J. *Behavior modification: Principles, issues, and applications.* Boston: Houghton Mifflin, 1976.

Critehly, M., & Henson, R. A. *Music and the brain: Studies in neurology of music.* London: William Heinemann Medical Books, 1977.

Deikman, A. J. Bimodal consciousness. *Archives of General Psychiatry,* 1971, *25,* 481–489.

De La Cruz, F., & La Veck, D. (Eds.). *Human sexuality and the mentally retarded.* New York: Brunner-Mazel, 1973.

Dentler, R. A., & Mackler, B. Originality: Some social and personal determinants. *Behavioral Science,* 1964, *9,* 1–7.

Deutscher, I. Words and deeds: Social science and social policy. *Social Problems,* 1966, *13.*

DeVillis, R. F. Learned helplessness in institutions. *Mental Retardation,* 1977, *15,* 10–13.

Dewey, J. *Art as experience.* New York: Minton, Balch, 1934.

Dodson, F. *How to Parent.* New York: New American Libarary, 1970.

Donn, L. M. (Ed.) *Exceptional children in the schools.* New York: Holt, Rinehart, and Winston, 1963.

Dreistadt, R. The psychology of creativity: How Einstein discovered the theory of relativity. *Psychology,* 1974, *11,* 15–25.

Edgerton, R. B. *The cloak of competence: Stigma in the lives of the mentally retarded.* Berkeley and Los Angeles: University of California Press, 1967.

_____. Issues relating to the quality of life among mentally retarded persons. In M. J. Begab & S. A. Richardson (Eds.) *The mentally retarded and society.* Baltimore: University Park Press, 1975.

Edgerton, R. B., & Bercovici, S. The cloak of competence: Years later. *American Journal of Mental Deficiency,* 1976, *80* (5), 485–497.

Edwards, B. *Drawing on the right side of the brain.* Los Angeles: J. P. Tarcher: 1979.

Einstein, A., & Infeld, L. *The evolution of physics.* New York: Simon & Schuster, 1938.

Farber, J. *Student as Nigger.* North Hollywood, Calif.: Contact Books, 1969.

Fields, S. Our common senses: Art therapy and therapeutic art. *Innovations,* Winter 1979, pp. 2–3.

Filstead, W. J. (Ed.). *Qualitative methodology: Firsthand involvement with the social world.* Chicago: Markam, 1970.

Fisher, L. L. Sexual development of the moderately retarded child: How can the pediatrician be helpful? *Clinical Pediatrics,* 1974, *13* (1), 79–83.

Fox, P. B. Locus of control and self-concept in mildly mentally retarded adolescents (Doctoral dissertation, University of Minnesota, 1972). *Dissertation Abstracts International,* 1972, *33,* 6–B.

Gaitskell, C. D., & Hurwitz, A. L. *Children and their art: Methods for the elementary school.* New York: Harcourt Brace Jovanovich, 1975.

Gallagher, P. A. Procedures for developing creativity in emotionally disturbed children. *Focus on Exceptional Children,* 1972, *4* (6), 3–12.

Gaston, T. E. *Music in therapy.* New York: Macmillan, 1968.

Gerald, H. B. Some effects of involvement upon evaluation. *Journal of Abnormal and Social Psychology,* 1958, *57.*

Ghiselin, B. *The creative process.* Berkeley: University of California Press, 1952.

Ginott, H. G. *Group psychotherapy with children.* New York: McGraw Hill, 1961.

———. *Between parent and child.* New York: Macmillan, 1965.

Glaser, B. G., & Strauss, A. *The discovery of grounded theory: Strategies for qualitative research.* Chicago: Aldine, 1967.

Goldman, L. (Ed.). *Research methods for counselors: Practical approaches in field settings.* New York: John Wiley & Sons, 1978.

Goodenough-Harris Drawing Test. New York: Harcourt Brace Jovanovich, 1963.

Gordon, T. *Parent effectiveness training.* New York: Peter A. Wyden, 1970.

Gould, R. *Child studies through fantasy.* New York: Quadrangle Books, 1972.

Grunewald, K. *The mentally retarded in Sweden.* Sweden: The Swedish Institute, 1974.

Haley, M. Contradictions in art education theory and practice. *Art Education,* 1956, *9* (5).

Hannan, R. W. A program for developing self-concept in retarded children. *Mental Retardation,* 1968, *69* (4), 33–37.

Harlow, H. F. The nature of love. In M. L. Haimowitz & N. R. Haimowitz (Eds.), *Human development: Selected readings.* New York: Thomas Y. Crowell, 1963.

Hayakawa, S. I. *Language in thought and action* (2nd ed.). New York: Harcourt, Brace & World, 1964.

Hayes, C. S., & Printz, R. J. Affective reactions of retarded and non-retarded children to success and failure. *American Journal of Mental Deficiency,* 1976, *81* (1), 100–102.

Heinig, R. B. S. *Creative dramatics for the classroom teacher.* Englewood Cliffs, N.J.: Prentice-Hall, 1974.

Heshusius, L. *Meaning in life as experienced by persons labeled retarded in a group home: A participant observation study.* Springfield, Ill.: Charles C. Thomas, 1981.

Hilgard, E. Impulsive versus realistic thinking: An examination of the distinction between primary and secondary process in thought. *Psychological Bulletin,* 1962, *59* (6), 477–488.

Hofstattler, L., & Hofstattler, L. Emotional problems of the child with mental retardation and his family. *Southern Medical Journal,* 1969, *62* (5), 583–587.

Huss, J. A. Touch with care or a caring touch? *American Journal of Occupational Therapy,* 1977, *30* (1), 11–18.

Jacobs, J. (Ed.). *Mental retardation: A phenomenological approach.* Springfield, Ill.: Charles C. Thomas, 1981.

Jessor, R. Phenomenological personality theories and data language of psychology. *Psychological Review,* 1956, *63* (3), 173–180.

Jourard, S. M. *Healthy personality: An approach from the viewpoint of humanistic psychology.* New York: Macmillan, 1974.

Kantor, K., & Perron, J. Thinking and writing: Creativity in the modes of discourse. *Language Arts,* 1977, *54* (7), 742–749.

Kaplan, A. Poetry, medicine and metaphysics. *Journal of the American Academy of Psychoanalysis*, 1981, *9* (1), 101–128.

Kase, R. C. *Stories for creative acting*. New York: Samuel French, 1961.

Kaur, R. Coping with a mentally retarded child. *Social Welfare*, 1977, *23* (10), 8.

Kessler, J. W., Ablon, G., & Smith, E. Separation reactions in young, mildly retarded children. *Children*, 1969, *16* (1), 2–7.

Klepac, R. L. Through the looking glass: Sociodrama and mentally retarded individuals. *Mental Retardation*, 1978, *16*, 343–345.

Koch, K. Teaching poetry to the old and ill. *Milbank Memorial Fund Quarterly / Health and Society*, 1978, *56* (1), 113–126.

Kocklemass, J. *First introduction to Husserl's phenomenology*. Pittsburgh: Duquesne University Press, 1967.

Kramer, E. *Art as therapy with children*. New York: Schocken Books, 1971.

Krippner, S. Subconsciousness and the creative process. *The Gifted Child Quarterly*, Autumn 1968, pp. 141–157.

Kurtz, P. D., & Neisworth, J. T. Self control possibilities for exceptional children. *Exceptional Children*, 1976, *42*, 212–216.

Lasswell, H. The social setting of creativity. In H. Anderson (Ed.), *Creativity and its cultivation*. New York: Harper, 1959, pp. 203–221.

Lawrence, E. A., & Winschel, J. F. Self-concept and the retarded: Research and issues. *Exceptional Children*, 1973, *39* (4), 310–319.

Leventhal, M. Movement therapy with minimal brain dysfunction children. In K. C. Mason (Ed.), *Dance Therapy* (Vol. 7). Focus on Dance. Washington, D.C.: American Association for Health, Physical Education, and Recreation, 1974.

Li, A. K. F. Play and the mentally retarded child. *Mental Retardation*, 1981, *19* (3), 121–127.

Linderman, E., Herberholtz, D. *Developing artistic and perceptual awareness*. Dubuque: William C. Brown, 1964.

Linderstrom, M. *Children's art*. Berkeley and Los Angeles: University of California Press, 1957.

Lopez, T. Psychotherapeutic assistance to a blind boy with limited intelligence. *Psychoanalytic Study of the Child*, 1974, *29*, 277–300.

Lovano-Kerr, J., & Savage, S. Incremental art curriculum model for the mentally retarded. *Exceptional Children*, 1972, *39* (3), 193–199.

Lowenfeld, B., & Brittain, W. L. *Creative and mental growth*. New York: Macmillan, 1964.

Luckey, R. E., & Chandler, P. J. Demonstration habilitative and self-care nursing projects for multi-handicapped retardates. *Mental Retardation*, 1968, *6* (5), 10–14.

McCaslin, N. *Creative dramatics in the classroom*. New York: Longman, Inc., 1974.

McEwen, J. L. Survey of attitudes toward sexual behavior of institutionalized mentally retarded. *Psychological Reports*, 1977, *41*, 874.

MacLeod, R. B. The phenomenological approach to social psychology. *Psychological Review*, 1947, *54*, 193–210.

Maehr, M., Mensing, J., & Nafzger, S. Concepts of self and the reaction of others. *Sociometry*, 1962, *25*, 352–357.

Mahoney, M. J., & Mahoney K. Self control techniques with the mentally retarded. *Exceptional Children*, 1976, *42*, 338–339.

Malinowski, B. Culture. In *Encyclopedia of Social Science* (Vol. 4). New York: Macmillan, 1931.

Mallenby, T. W. A note on perceived self-acceptance of institutionalized retarded (TMR) children. *Journal of Genetic Psychology*, 1973, *123*, 171–172.

_____. Personal space: Projective and direct measures with institutionalized mentally retarded children. *Journal of Personality Assessment*, 1974, *38* (1), 28–31.

Maltzman, I. On the training of originality. *Psychological Review*, 1960, *67*, 229–242.

Maslow, A. H. *Motivation and personality*. New York: Harper, 1954.

_____. *The farther reaches of human nature*. New York: The Viking Press, 1971.

May, R. *The courage to create*. New York: W. W. Norton, 1975.

Menolascino, F. J. Emotional disturbances in mentally retarded children. *Archives of General Psychiatry*, 1969, *126* (2), 168–176.

Miller, W. R. Psychological deficit in depression. *Psychological Bulletin*, 1975, *82*, 2, 238–260.

Montague, A. Sociogenic brain damage. *American Anthropologist*, 1972, *74*, 1045–1061.

Montague, J. C., & Cage, B. N. Self concepts of institutional and non-institutional educable mentally retarded children. *Perceptual and Motor Skills*, 1974, *38*, 977–978.

Mora, G. One hundred years from Lombroso's first essay "genius and insanity." *The American Journal of Psychiatry*, 1964, *121*, 562–571.

Morena, D. A., & Litrownik, A. J. Self-concept in educable mentally retarded and emotionally handicapped children. *Journal of Abnormal Child Psychology*, 1974, *2* (4), 281–292.

Mott, D., Rosenkoetter, J., & Stamatelos, T. *Emotional needs of persons with mental retardation: A preliminary review*. Washington, D.C.: National Mental Health Association, 1981.

Naroll, R., & Cohen, R. *Handbook of method in cultural anthropology*. Garden City, N.Y.: Natural History Press, 1970.

Nash, B. C., & McQuisten, A. Self-concepts of senior TMR students at a semi-integrated setting. *Mental Retardation*, 1977, *15*, 16–18.

Nesbett, R. E., & Wilson, T. D. Telling more than we can know: verbal reports on mental process. *Psychological Review*, 1977, *84* (3), 231–259.

Nirje, B. The normalization principle: Implications and comments. *Journal of Mental Subnormality* (Birmingham, England), 1970, *16* (31), 62–70.

Nixon, B. L. Imagine that! *School and Community*, September 1979, p. 23.

Novak, B. J., Wicas, E. A., & Ellias, G. S. The school counselor and retarded youth—opportunity or threat? *Personnel and Guidance Journal*, 1977, *56* (3), 131–133.

Ogletree, E. J. Eurythmy: A therapeutic art of movement. *Journal of Special Education*, 1976, *10* (3), 305–319.

Olfson, Lewy. *Pantomime*. New York: Sterling, 1971.

Orem, R. C. *Montessori and the special child*. New York: G. P. Putnam's Sons, 1969.

Ornstein, Robert. *The mind fields*. New York: Pocket Books, 1976.

Parnes, S. *Creativity: Unlocking human potential*. New York: D.O.K., 1972.

Patrick, C. Creative thought in poets. *Archives of Psychology*, 1935, *26*, 1-74.

_____. Creative thought in artists. *Journal of Psychology*, 1938, *4*, 35-73.

_____. Painting and personality. *Rorschach Research Exchange*, 1946, *10*, 86-100.

Payne, J. E. The effects of institutionalization on educable mental retardates' expectance of failure. *Training School Bulletin*, 1971, *68* (2), 77-81.

Pease, D. *Creative writing in the elementary school: Psychology and technique*. Hicksville, N.Y.: Exposition Press, 1964.

Perrine, L. *Sound and sense: An introduction to poetry*. New York: Harcourt, Brace and World, 1956.

Perske, R. About sexual development: An attempt to be human with the mentally retarded. *Mental Retardation*, 1973, *11* (1), 6-8.

Philips, I. Psychopathology and mental retardation. *American Journal of Psychiatry*, 1967, *124* (1), 29-35.

Philipson, M. *Outline of Jungian aesthetics*. Evanston, Ill.: Northwestern University Press, 1963.

Piaget, Jean. *Play, dreams and imitations in childhood*. New York: W. W. Norton, 1962.

Pilulski, J. Initiating creative writing activities. *Elementary English*, 1975, *52*, 183-186.

Pitcher, E. G., & Prelinger, E. *Children tell stories*. New York: International Universities Press, 1963.

Power, P. W., & Marinelli, R. P. Normalization and the sheltered workshop: a review and proposals for change. *Rehabilitation Literature*, 1974, *35* (3), 66-72.

Reinhardt, J. B., & Brash, A. L. Psychosocial dwarfism: Environmentally induced recovery. *Psychosomatic Medicine*, 1969, *31*, 165-172.

Risley, T. R. Behavior modification: An experimental-therapeutic endeavor. In L. A. Hammerlynck, P. O. Davidson, & L. E. Acker (Eds.), *Behavior modification and ideal mental health services*. Calgary, Canada: University of Calgary Press, 1973, pp. 103-127.

Robinson, H. B., & Robinson, L. H. Mental retardation. In P. H. Munsen (Ed.), *Carmichael's Manual of Child Psychology* (3rd ed.). New York: John Wiley & Sons, 1970.

Robinson, L. H. Therapeutic tutoring of retarded adolescents by medical students. *Journal of the American Academy of Child Psychiatry*, 1976, *15* (2), 243-356.

Robinson, N. M., & Robinson, H. B. Psychotherapy with the mentally retarded. In N. M. Robinson & H. B. Robinson (Eds.), *The mentally retarded child* (2nd ed.). New York: McGraw-Hill, 1976.

Roe, A. The personality of artists. *Educational Psychological Measurement*, 1946, *6*, 401-408.

Rogers, C. Some observations on the organization of personality. *American Psychologist*, 1947, *2*, 358-368.

_____. *Client-centered therapy: Its current practice, implications and theory.* Boston: Houghton Mifflin, 1951.

_____. *Becoming a person.* Oberlin College Nellie Heldt Lecture Series. Oberlin, O.: Oberlin College, 1954. (a)

_____. Toward a theory of creativity. *Review of General Semantics,* 1954, *11* (4), 249-260. (b)

_____. On becoming a person. Boston: Houghton Mifflin, 1961.

_____. *Freedom to learn.* Columbus, O.: Charles E. Merrill, 1969.

_____. *On personal power.* New York: Delacorte, 1977.

Roos, P. Normalization, de-humanization and conditioning: Conflict or harmony? *Mental Retardation,* 1970, *8* (4), 12-14.

Roos, P., & McCann, B. M. Major trends in mental retardation. *Introductory Journal of Mental Health,* 1977, *6* (1), 3-20.

Rosen, H. G., & Rosen, S. Group therapy as an instrument to develop a concept of self-worth in the adolescent and young adult mentally retarded. *Mental Retardation,* 1969, *7* (5), 52-55.

Roser, N. L., & Britt, J. Writing with flair. *Elementary English,* 1975, *52.*

Rosenkoetter, J. L. Self-concept and the mentally retarded: Implications for intervention. Unpublished manuscript, 1980.

Rosenthal, R., & Rosnow, R. (Eds.). *Artifacts in behavioral research.* New York: Academic Press, 1969.

Rubin, B. Handbells in therapy. *Journal of Music Therapy.* 1976, *13* (1), 49-53.

Rychlak, J. F. Is a concept of "self" necessary in psychological theory, and if so why? A humanistic perspective. In A. Wandersman, P. J. Poppen, and D. F. Ricks (Eds.), *Humanism and behaviorism: Dialogue and growth.* New York: Pergamon Press, 1976.

Schachtel, E. G. On creative experience. *Journal of Association of Humanistic Psychologists,* 1971, *11* (1), 26-39.

Schurr, K. T., Joiner, L. M., & Towne, R. C. Self-concept research on the mentally retarded: A review of empirical studies. *Mental Retardation,* 1970, *8,* 39-43.

Schuster, S. O., & Gruen, G. E. Success and failure as determinants of the performance predictions of the mentally retarded and non-retarded children. *American Journal of Mental Deficiency,* 1971, *76* (2), 190-196.

Segy, L. Geometric art and aspects of reality: A phenomenological approach. *Centennial Review,* 1967, *11,* 419-455.

Selan, B. H. Psychotherapy with the developmentally disabled. *Health and Social Work,* 1976, *1* (1), 73-85.

Selwa, B. I. Preliminary consideration in psychotherapy with retarded children. *Journal of School Psychology,* 1971, *9* (1), 12-15.

Siks, G. B. *Children's literature for dramatization: An anthology.* New York: Harper and Row, 1964.

Simpson, H. M., & Meaney, C. Effects of learning to ski on the self-concept of mentally retarded children. *American Journal of Mental Deficiency,* 1979, *84* (1), 25-29.

Sindell, P. Anthropological approaches to the study of education. *Review of Educational Research,* 1969, *39,* 593-607.

Singer, J. L. Imagination and writing ability in young children. *Journal of Personality*, 1961, *29*, 396–413.

Skipper, C. E., & DeVelbiss, J. A. Developing creative abilities in adolescents. *Innovations in Education*, November 1969, pp. 191–193.

Smith, B. The phenomenological approach in personality theory: Some critical remarks. *Journal of Abnormal and Social Psychology*, 1950, *45*, 516–522.

Smith, J., and Perks, W. *Humanism and the arts in special education*. Albuquerque: University of New Mexico, Bureau of Education for the Handicapped, 1978.

Snygg, D., & Combs, A. W. *Individual behavior: A new frame of reference for psychology*. New York: Harper, 1949.

Spolin, V. *Improvisation for the theater*. Evanston, Ill.: Northwestern University Press, 1963.

Srouf, L. A. Socioemotional development. In J. R. Oshofsky (Ed.), *Handbook of infant development*. New York: John Wiley & Sons, 1979.

Stabler, J., Stabler, J. O., & Karger, R. H. Evaluation of paintings of nonretarded and retarded persons by judges with and without art training. *American Journal of Mental Deficiency*, 1977, *81* (5), 502–503.

Stacey, C. L., & DeMartino, M. F. *Counseling and psychotherapy with the mentally retarded*. Glencoe, Ill.: Free Press, 1957.

Stamatelos, T., & Mott, D. Creative writing as a method to structure emotional habilitation in a mildly retarded institutionalized male. Paper presented at the Annual Conference of the American Association on Mental Deficiency, Boston, 1982. (a)

_____. Humanism and mental retardation: Current and future perspectives. Paper presented at the Annual Conference of the American Association on Mental Deficiency, Boston, 1982. (b)

_____. Learned helplessness in mentally retarded people: Art as a client-centered treatment modality. Paper presented at the Annual Conference of the American Association on Mental Deficiency, Boston, 1982. (c)

Sternlicht, M., & Wexler, H. K. Cathartic tension reduction in the retarded: An experimental demonstration. *American Journal of Mental Deficiency*, 1966, *70* (4), 609–611.

Strang, L., Smith, M. D., & Rogers, C. M. Social comparison, multiple reference groups, and the self-concept of academically handicapped children before and after mainstreaming. *Journal of Educational Psychology*, 1978, *70* (4), 487–497.

Szymanski, L. S., & Tanguay, P. E. *Emotional disorders of mentally retarded persons*. Baltimore: University Park Press, 1980.

Taylor, C. W. (Ed.). *Creativity: Progress and potential*. New York: McGraw-Hill, 1963.

Terwilliger, P. N., & Turner, T. N. I hate you, Dr. T.: A creative approach that knocks the sails out of your wind! *Elementary English*, 1975, *52* (2), 170–173.

Thursby, D. D. Everyone's a star. *Teaching Exceptional Children*, Spring 1975, pp. 77–78.

Torrance, E. P. *Guiding creative talent*. Englewood Cliffs, N.J.: Prentice-Hall, 1962.

_____. *What research says to the teacher: Creativity.* Washington, D.C.: Department of Classroom Teachers, American Research Association of the National Education Association, 1963.

Torrance, E. P., & Myers, R. E. *Creative learning and teaching.* New York: Dodd, Mead, 1972.

Tway, E. Creative writing: From gimmick to goal. *Elementary English,* 1975, *52* (2), 173-174.

Vidich, A. Participant observation and the collection and interpretation of data. *American Journal of Sociology,* 1955, *60,* 354-360.

Wade, S. Differences between intelligence and creativity: Some speculations on the role of environment. *The Journal of Creative Behavior,* 1967, *1,* 283-290.

Weiner, K. From out of the past — Old time radio rides again. *Teaching Exceptional Children,* Summer 1974, pp. 210-213.

Willenson, D., & Bisgaard, S. P.E.T. for psychiatric technicians in state institutions for the mentally retarded. Unpublished manuscript, 1970.

Williems, E. P. Planning a rationale for naturalistic research. In E. P. Williems & H. L. Raush (Eds.), *Naturalistic viewpoints in psychological research.* New York: Holt, Rinehart and Winston, 1969.

Wilson, L. Theory and practice of art therapy with the mentally retarded. *American Journal of Art Therapy,* 1977, *16,* 87-97.

Wilson, S. The use of ethnographic techniques in educational research. *Review of Educational Research,* 1977, *47* (1), 245-265.

Wolfensberger, W. *The principles of normalization in human services.* Toronto: National Institute on Mental Retardation, 1972.

Wylie, R. C. *The self concept: A critical survey of pertinent research literature.* Lincoln: University of Nebraska Press, 1961.

Zigler, E. Research on personality structures in the retardate. In N. R. Ellis (Ed.), *International review of research in mental retardation* (Vol. 1). New York: Academic Press, 1966.

_____. The retarded child as a whole person. In D. K. Routh (Ed.), *The experimental psychology of mental retardation.* Chicago: Aldine, 1973, pp. 231-322.

Zigler, E. D., Balla, D., & Watson, N. Developmental and experimental determinants of self-image disparity in institutionalized and noninstitutionalized retarded and normal children. *Journal of Personality and Social Psychology,* 1972, *23,* (1), 81-87.

Zukav, Gary. *The dancing Wu-Li masters: An overview of the new physics.* New York: William Morrow, 1979.

Index